Library of
Davidson College

TAXES, SUBSIDIES

and Competitiveness Internationally

BY JOHN MUTTI
Associate Professor of Economics
University of Wyoming

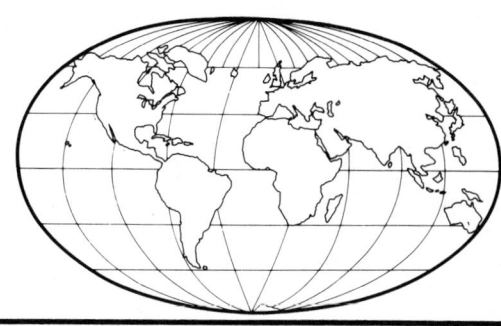

NPA Committee on
Changing International Realities

338.97
M993t

Taxes, Subsidies and Competitiveness Internationally

CIR Report #11
NPA Report #191

Price $7.00

ISBN 0-89068-062-0
Library of Congress
Catalog Card Number 81-86163

Copyright January 1982
by NPA
A voluntary association incorporated under the laws of
the District of Columbia
1606 New Hampshire Avenue, N.W.
Washington, D.C. 20009

 82-1825

Contents

Taxes, Subsidies and Competitiveness Internationally

by John Mutti

NPA's Committee on Changing International Realities and Their Implications for U.S. Policy		inside front cover
A Statement by the Committee on Changing International Realities		v
Members of the Committee Signing the Statement		vii
Chapter 1	**Introduction**	1
Chapter 2	**A Fiscal Balance at the Aggregate Level**	5
	Taxes	5
	National Tax Structures	5
	Neutrality in the Impacts of Different Taxes among Industries	7
	Subsidies	9
	Operating Subsidies	9
	Capital Subsidies	11
	Research and Development Subsidies	12
	Export Subsidies	12
	Aggregate Fiscal Balance	13
Chapter 3	**Industry Studies**	17
	The Textile Industry	18
	The Steel Industry	24
	The Automotive Industry: Passenger Cars	31
	The Pharmaceutical Industry	36
	The Computer Industry	41
Chapter 4	**Summary and Conclusions**	50

Appendix A	Summary of Tax and Subsidy Programs, and Historical Trade Data	54
Appendix B	Modeling International Competitive Effects of Tax and Subsidy Policies	57
Appendix C	Assessing a Proposed Value-Added Tax	59
	Selected Bibliography	62
	NPA	65
	NPA Officers and Board of Trustees	66
	Recent NPA International Publications	*inside back cover*

TABLES

Chapter 2	1. Tax Revenues as a Percentage of GDP, 1976	6
	2. Aggregate Indicators of Government Subsidy Policies as a Percentage of GDP, 1976	10
	3. A General Balance of Tax and Subsidy Policies as a Percentage of GDP, 1976	14
Chapter 3	4. Comparative Textile Industry Statistics	20
	5. Comparative Steel Industry Statistics, 1977	25
	6. Comparative Passenger Car Statistics, 1977	32
	7. Comparative Pharmaceutical Industry Statistics	37
	8. Comparative Computer Industry Statistics	42
Appendix A	A-1. International Tax Systems and Incentives, 1978	54
	A-2. Grants and Capital Subsidies, 1978	56

A Statement by the Committee on Changing International Realities

Since its establishment, the Committee on Changing International Realities (CIR) has been concerned with domestic and international factors affecting the competitive position of American industry. In an era of rising costs for imported resources and growing export capacities in new and traditional centers of industrial activity, the state of U.S. competitiveness is an important factor in determining the adequacy and quality of employment opportunities and the standards of living Americans can aspire to now, and in the future.

Today, the contribution of government policies to the less-than-encouraging record of recent U.S. domestic and international economic performance is at the center of public debate, as proposals for policy changes intended to impact the supply side of the economic equation, such as investment, productivity and labor-force participation, are evaluated by advisers to the new administration. Good performance in these areas is vital to the maintenance and improvement of U.S. competitiveness. The CIR has sought to play a constructive role by sponsoring a series of studies on the economic factors and government policies affecting U.S. competitiveness.

This study, by Professor John Mutti, is the fifth in the series and compares taxes and subsidies impacting U.S. industry with similiar policies in six other major industrial countries. An assessment of subsidies, as well as taxes, is essential to obtain a balanced and accurate understanding of the impact of fiscal policies on international competitiveness.

For example, the author estimates that U.S. taxes levied on labor and capital are relatively low—higher than Japan but lower than Canada, France, Germany, Italy, and the United Kingdom. But when estimates of the value of government programs that directly or indirectly subsidize the productive uses of labor and capital, such as aids to capital formation and R&D expenditures, are added to the analysis, the U.S. position does not look as good. The data indicate that the net benefits provided labor and capital (taxes less subsidies) in the U.S. industrial sector are lower in terms of percent of gross national product than in any of the six other countries studied.

As sobering as these results are, they should not be interpreted so as to assign tax and subsidy policies sole or even dominant responsibility for the U.S. competitive performance because the effects of these policies can vary substantially across the sectors of the economy. Therefore, Professor Mutti also examines the effects of taxes and subsidies on competitive performance in five industries—textiles, steel, automobiles, pharmaceuticals, and computers. He finds that although the fiscal policies of the United States and other industrial countries have had some effect on U.S. performance, other policies by foreign governments, such as import constraints, government procurement and regulation, have probably been more important; hence the necessity to examine the full range of government policies when assessing their contribution to competitive performance.

We believe that, at this crucial point in the evolution of the U.S. economy, careful evaluations of the full range of U.S. domestic and international economic policies and the interrelationships between them are crucial. The data and analysis provided by Dr. Mutti's study should substantially contribute to this effort and are worthy of the attention of private- and public-sector decisionmakers and concerned citizens. Accordingly, regardless of whether we agree or disagree with all of the study's specific interpretations and conclusions, we believe it makes an important contribution to our understanding of the economic policy questions confronting the nation. We are therefore pleased to recommend that it be published by NPA as a report signed by its author.

This paper emphasizes some important aspects of international realities, including the difficulties of drawing general conclusions from international comparisons. The author explains very well that foreign trade barriers and other institutional arrangements may overshadow the more obvious and more easily quantified factors, such as tax rates and direct government subsidies. The discussion of the potential impact on trade flows of different government and industry arrangements in other countries is useful as a basis for public discussion. Hopefully, others will be encouraged to examine many of these issues more closely.

In particular, I feel that further analyses will indicate that taxes and subsidies are far more disruptive and important than the present study indicates. It is unfortunate that economists seem unable to recognize that the combination of trade barriers and governmental intervention, with taxes and subsidies, may be the biggest changing international reality that the United States must face. Even though I cannot agree with all of the policy statements and conclusions, I think this paper should be published. — **Ernest S. Lee**

Members of the Committee on Changing International Realities Signing the Statement

J.G. CLARKE
Chairman; Director & Senior Vice President, Exxon Corporation

ROBERT R. FREDERICK
Chairman of the Executive Committee; Executive Vice President & Sector Executive of International Sector, General Electric Company

JOHN MILLER
Secretary; Vice Chairman and Acting President, NPA

LEE S. APPLETON
Regional Vice President, East Allis-Chalmers Corporation

HOWARD W. BELL
Director & Financial Vice President, Standard Oil Company of California

RICHARD M. BISSELL, JR.
Consultant, The Exchange

JOHN C. BROOMAN
President & Chief Operating Officer, The Black and Decker Manufacturing Company

G.A. COSTANZO
New York, New York

J.W. DAVISON
Senior Vice President, Phillips Petroleum Company

MURRAY H. FINLEY
President, Amalgamated Clothing and Textile Workers' Union

RAYMOND G. FISHER
Business Consultant, Greenwich, Connecticut

THEODORE GEIGER
Distinguished Research Professor of Intersocietal Relations, School of Foreign Service, Georgetown University

ROGER W. GRAY
Professor & Economist, Food Research Institute, Stanford University

JOHN H. JACKSON
Professor of Law, The University of Michigan Law School

G. GRIFFITH JOHNSON, JR.
Executive Vice President, Motion Picture Association of America, Inc.

LEONARD KAMSKY
Senior Vice President, W.R. Grace and Company

TOM KILLEFER
Chairman of the Board & Chief Executive Officer, United States Trust Company of New York

PETER F. KROGH
Dean, Edmund A. Walsh School of Foreign Service, Georgetown University

*ERNEST S. LEE
Director, Department of International Affairs, AFL-CIO

WILLIAM R. MILLER
Executive Vice President, Bristol-Myers Company

ALFRED F. MIOSSI
Executive Vice President, Continental Illinois National Bank & Trust Company of Chicago

WILLIAM S. OGDEN
Vice Chairman & Chief Financial Officer, The Chase Manhattan Bank, N.A.

WILLIAM R. PEARCE
Corporate Vice President, Cargill Incorporated

RALPH A. PFEIFFER, JR.
Chairman of the Board, IBM, World Trade Americas/Far East Corporation

CHARLES J. PILLIOD, JR.
Chairman of the Board, Goodyear Tire & Rubber Company

THOMAS A. REED
Group Vice President, Honeywell Inc.

JERRY REES
Executive Vice President, National Association of Wheat Growers

NATHANIEL SAMUELS
Chairman, Advisory Board, Lehman Brothers Kuhn Loeb, Inc. & Chairman, Olivetti Corporation of America

DANIEL I. SARGENT
General Partner, Salomon Brothers

MARK SHEPHERD, JR.
Chairman of the Board & Chief Executive Officer, Texas Instruments Inc.

---

* See footnote to the Statement.

Committee Signers

WILLIAM F. SPENGLER
President & Chief Operating Officer, Domestic Operations, Owens-Illinois

RALPH I. STRAUS
New York, New York

WALTER STERLING SURREY
Senior Partner, Surrey & Morse

THOMAS N. URBAN
President & Chief Executive Officer, Pioneer Hi-Bred International

MARK H. WILLES
Executive Vice President & Chief Financial Officer, General Mills, Inc.

RALPH S. YOHE
Editor, *Wisconsin Agriculturist*

The opinions expressed and the recommendations presented in the Committee Statement are solely those of the individual members of the Committee on Changing International Realities whose signatures are offered hereto and do not represent the views of NPA or its staff. Committee members' agreement or disagreement with specific points of this statement is expressed in signed footnotes.

Introduction 1

The multilateral tariff reductions achieved in the Kennedy Round trade negotiations carried out in the late 1960s and early '70s promised a much freer system of international trade. However, with the reduction of tariffs, the importance of nontariff forms of government intervention in determining trade flows has become more apparent. In fact, tariff reductions may even have accelerated the growth of nontariff restrictions of trade as the interest groups previously protected by tariffs have appealed to governments for other forms of support.

Two key forms of government support are direct expenditures or subsidies that benefit an industry, and forgiveness of tax obligations that otherwise would be incurred. The purpose of the present study is to consider the effects of tax and subsidy policies on international competitiveness more broadly, not merely to examine those policies adopted in response to recent trade conditions. Major emphasis will be placed on the recent thrust of policies in seven major industrialized countries: Canada, France, (West) Germany, Italy, Japan, the United Kingdom, and the United States.

The importance of government intervention through tax and subsidy measures increasingly has attracted attention in the United States, as foreigners have made inroads into traditional U.S. export markets and into the U.S. domestic market. Periodic concern over the U.S. trade deficit has been expressed. U.S. producers have long had the opportunity to petition the Treasury Department to impose countervailing duties on imports when government subsidies to trade result in a competitive advantage for foreign producers. Yet, from the establishment of this provision in 1897 until 1967, no countervailing duty was ever levied.[1] Only more recently have they been imposed and still rather sparingly. A particularly noteworthy case was the determination in 1973 that countervailing duties could be imposed against exports from a Michelin tire plant in Nova Scotia.[2] Thus, a subsidy program allegedly motivated on the grounds of regional economic development and equity within Canada was judged to be a direct grant or bounty to foreign trade since more than 80 percent of the plant's output was exported to the United States. That decision was made unilaterally by the United States, but a major provision of the Tokyo Round of Multilateral Trade Negotiations (MTN) concluded in 1979 is a new countervailing duty code covering not only direct subsidies to exports but also domestic subsidies that indirectly affect exports. These domestic policies are not explicitly listed in the code, and the cost of obtaining this concession was the U.S. acceptance of a material injury test. Yet, the U.S. bargaining position would seem to imply that American producers will be able to obtain countervailing duty relief in many trade-impacted industries that face strong import competition. At the same time, the way in which these provisions are applied may have serious adverse consequences for countries with small national markets, which are forced to export large proportions of whatever they produce to achieve necessary economies of scale.

The United States is not the only country concerned with the trade implications of such domestic policies. The Commission of the European Community has the right to review and judge the compatibility of state aids, such as investment and job incentives, with the purposes of the EC, as well as to rule on complaints brought by private firms against the practices of member countries. While a large number of complaints have been resolved through private negotiations without making the details public, many decisions have been made that predate the 1973 Michelin case. For instance, in 1970 the Commission ruled that an Italian law to restructure Italy's textile sector could not include a 10-year tax exemption from any direct taxes on income from new investment.[3] More recently established standards deal with the maximum aid to be made available to new investments or jobs created and also with the design of export promotion schemes. Some of these limitations imposed by the Commission on the degree of permissible subsidization by member states have benefited countries outside the EC by reducing the extent to which all countries must compete with subsidized producers. In general, though, the actions of the Commission have a much narrower focus, aimed at preventing distortions in competition within the Community.

These developments suggest that trade policy discussions will come to include a much wider class of concerns than previously. A review of tax and subsidy policies not directed explicitly at trade flows is a relevant starting point. A summary is presented in this study from two perspectives, one at a very aggregate level and the other at the industry level, based on analysis of the textile, steel, pharmaceutical, automobile, and computer industries. At the aggregate level, a general indication is given to tax and subsidy programs that affect the costs of producing goods generally, as contrasted to measures designed specifically to aid particular sectors. Government intervention through taxation generally adds to the costs of operation, while tax exemptions, subsidies, grants, and direct provision of services reduce costs that otherwise would have been faced.

In considering national tax systems, the total tax burden and its division among various types of taxes are presented for international comparison as percentages of national product in each country. A distinction between direct taxes on income and indirect taxes on products has become particularly significant in recent trade policy debates, as exemplified by the Zenith TV case ruled on by the U.S. Supreme Court in 1978. In that case, Zenith claimed that Japanese rebates to exporters of a TV commodity tax constituted a bounty or grant; the court ruled against Zenith. A possible implication from the case still to be considered is whether a change in current international border-tax adjustment procedures toward comparable treatment of direct and indirect taxes would necessarily work to the advantage of the United States. The aggregate figures reported are useful in suggesting an answer. Another tax-related issue is whether the United States should adopt a value-added tax (VAT) and reduce the relative importance of direct taxes such as social security or the corporate income tax. The aggregate figures reported suggest that production and trade patterns would probably be altered. This finding rests on a somewhat technical analysis that is developed in Appendix C.

With respect to direct government subsidies, the easiest aspect to capture is that which refers to current account payments. Common examples are expenditures to cover operating deficits of government enterprises or to make more attractive private output in sectors such as shipbuilding, coal mining or agriculture. Less directly measurable are grants and loans made on favorable terms for long-term capital expenditures by public and private enterprises. In the case of publicly owned enterprises, this form of aid often occurs through the government purchase of additional shares of stock. Another aspect of capital subsidy is in export financing, particularly of goods and equipment to be paid for over several years. A 1976 accord among developed countries, subsequently modified in 1981 to raise minimum lending rates to 10 percent, still leaves plenty of scope for concessional export sales in the current inflationary situation. Other government expenditures, such as those to provide services, training, research and development, or infrastructure at less than cost, also affect private production costs; their amounts are estimated. Subsidy figures fail to capture other ways in which government intervention can affect production costs through rules and regulations regarding safety and health standards, environmental controls and so on. Those issues are considered to some extent in the specific industry analyses in Chapter 3, but no reasonable generalizations can be made at an aggregate level.

The aggregate tax and subsidy figures for a country give very rough indications of the impact of fiscal policies on production costs. Ways in which the joint effect of these policies may alter the international competitive positions of producers in the various countries are considered in the first section of the study. While simplifying assumptions must be imposed to project precisely how these tax and subsidy provisions will affect costs, international production and the volume of trade of each country, the conclusion nevertheless emerges that U.S. producers on average receive considerably fewer fiscal benefits than most major foreign producers.

All producers do not experience the same impact as the average effect estimated at the national level. The third chapter of this study deals with the effects of tax and subsidy policies in five industries: textiles, steel, automobiles, pharmaceuticals, and computers. Those policies considered particularly favor or penalize one industry relative to others. The general tax and subsidy policies outlined above take on varying degrees of importance in these five industries, which were selected because of the quite different situations they represent. In the case of textiles, nearly every country studied has adopted some plan to aid its domestic producers, even as overall capacity is reduced; government intervention in trade agreements has been substantial, while government ownership is minor. By contrast, rationalization schemes in the steel industry often have been carried out in essentially nationalized industries. Neither of these industries have as much direct foreign investment as the remaining three industries. Measures affecting foreign investment include tax provisions dealing with foreign earned income, along with the set of domestic tax incentives, favorable loan conditions and outright grants available when new plants are established. In industries requiring relatively large R&D outlays, such as pharmaceuticals and computers, special research grants and tax concessions must be considered. Direct government grants to cover development costs are particularly important as many governments appear to have adopted the goal of ensuring that nationalized firms are maintained as viable enterprises in prestige industries such as automobiles and computers. The amount of support required may be considerable in these cases, particularly when the domestic market provides an inadequate scale of operations over which to spread high fixed costs of research, redesign and modernization.

Of course, the impact of tax and subsidy policies may be only a minor determinant of international competitiveness compared to other forms of government intervention, such as the imposition of tariffs and quotas that directly restrain trade or the various regulations noted above that can limit the potential to trade; some of these trade impediments may dictate foreign investment in the target country's market. For the five industries studies, an attempt is made to indicate the situations where these factors seem to play a dominant role.

In summary, this group of industry studies is designed to investigate tax and subsidy policies that are intended to favor particular industries and that can affect the location of their production internationally. However, projecting the consequent international competitive effects is not a straightforward exercise. Making that link, especially with respect to the impact on U.S. producers and domestic output, is a necessary second step in each industry study and serves as the focus of the concluding chapter.

Notes

1   Richard Cooper, "U.S. Policies and Practices on Subsidies in International Trade," in *International Trade and Industrial Policies,* ed., Steven Warnecke (New York: Holmes and Meier, 1978), p. 114.

2   Ibid.

3   Commission of the European Communities, *Second Report on Competition Policy* (Brussels, 1973), pp. 87–88.

A Fiscal Balance at the Aggregate Level 2

TAXES

National Tax Structures

If higher taxes result in higher production costs in a country, then national tax policies can affect international competitiveness. However, not all taxes necessarily affect production costs in the same way. Furthermore, the way in which taxes are imposed on goods traded internationally depends on the type of tax levied. A numerical summary is presented in Table 1 indicating the relative importance of various taxes as a percentage of gross domestic product in the seven countries studied. It is evident that tax structures vary considerably across countries.

The table shows that the four European countries have the greatest total tax burden as a percentage of GNP, followed by Canada, the United States and Japan. That Germany and Japan rank so differently suggests that the size of total tax burdens is not a good basis for predicting international competitiveness since both countries are generally recognized as being highly competitive.

The importance of indirect taxes is higher in the four European countries and Canada than in the United States and Japan. The value-added tax imposed on most transactions in Europe accounts for this difference. In 1976, the normal VAT rate was 20 percent in France, 12 percent in Italy, 11 percent in Germany, and 8 percent in the United Kingdom.[1] Consequently, the number one ranking accorded France regarding the importance of indirect taxes is not surprising. Even though Canada has no value-added tax, it ranks higher than the United States in this category largely due to a federal manufacturer's tax and to the greater importance of import duties.

With respect to direct taxes, the same general groupings exist as in the case of total tax burdens: the four European countries rank highest, followed by Canada, the United States and Japan. There is considerable diversity in the relative importance of different direct taxes. France, Italy and Germany rely more heavily on social security contributions than the other four countries. The Organization for Economic Cooperation and Development (OECD) reports that the joint employee-employer social security payment in 1978 from an average manufacturing worker in these countries was 51.2 percent of wage income in France, 50.4 percent in Italy and 31.4 percent in Germany.[2] Conversely, noncorporate (largely personal) income taxes are more important in the United Kingdom, Canada and the United States. Germany ranks high in both categories. Comparisons in terms of an average worker, as cited in the OECD report, are more difficult because distinctions must be made for the number of dependents the worker claims; in any case, using a single income and payment figure gives no indication of the progressivity of the tax structure. As a very rough indication of the relative importance of personal income taxes, a single worker making the average wage would pay 24.2 percent of his or her income as personal income tax in the United Kingdom, 19.0 percent in the United States, 18.9 percent in Canada, and 18.2 percent in Germany.[3]

TABLE 1: TAX REVENUES AS A PERCENTAGE OF GDP, 1976

	Total Taxes	Indirect Taxes[1]	Social Security[2]		Direct Taxes				Total[6] Direct
			Employee	Employer	Corporate Income	Noncorporate Income[3]	Property[4]	Other[5]	
Canada	32.89	10.49		3.46	3.86	11.25	3.08	0.49	22.14
France	39.45	12.79	3.56	11.32	2.28	4.95	1.51	2.03	25.65
Germany	36.70	9.45	5.60	6.87	1.69	11.08	1.20	0.56	27.00
Italy	35.82	10.07	3.19	13.23	2.23	5.91	1.19	—	25.75
Japan	20.19	3.97	1.96	2.74	3.48	5.13	1.92	1.07	16.31
United Kingdom	36.70	9.35	2.85	4.08	1.72	13.97	4.45	0.08	27.15
United States	29.29	5.30	2.86	4.14	3.02	9.68	4.09	—	23.79

[1]Includes general sales, value-added and specific excise taxes.
[2]Includes contributions of employers, employees and the self-employed. The category is broadly defined to include all tax payments to institutions of general government providing social welfare benefits, if levied as a function of pay or a fixed amount per person. Thus, for the United States, this category includes contributions to the railroad retirement fund, unemployment insurance fund, workmen's compensation fund, and civil service retirement program, in addition, of course, to the more familiar social security-type payments made pursuant to the Federal Insurance Contributions Act (FICA).
[3]Includes income taxes on individual and unincorporated enterprises such as proprietorships and partnerships.
[4]Includes taxes on net wealth and immovable property. Thus, for the United States, this category would be made up largely of state and local taxes on real and personal property.
[5]Includes taxes on employers based on payroll or manpower, taxes and stamp duties on gifts, inheritances and capital or financial transactions, motor vehicle license fees, and miscellaneous taxes.
[6]Total direct taxes derived as the sum of individual entries, but this figure plus indirect taxes may not yield the total tax figure, apparently due to rounding errors.
Source: OECD, *Revenue Statistics of OECD Member Countries, 1965–76.*

In all countries, the corporate income tax is a less important source of revenue than either payroll taxes or personal income taxes, which are relatively more important in Japan, Canada and the United States. These national differences are somewhat surprising given the statutory rates imposed in the seven countries. General national corporate income tax rates applicable in 1976 were: the United Kingdom, 52 percent; Germany, 51 percent; France, 50 percent; the United States, 48 percent; Canada, 46 percent; Japan, 40 percent; and Italy, 35 percent.[4] When the local corporate taxes reported are included, the statutory rates appear quite similar.[5]

A major reason for differences in the ratios of corporate tax receipts to gross domestic product is the relative importance of the corporate sector in the economy. In countries where public ownership is high, or where an important role is played by sole proprietorships or partnerships such as family farms and retail businesses, corporate profits and income tax payments will be less important. OECD statistics for 1976 indicate the following shares of corporate income in national income: Canada, 9.2 percent; Japan, 7.7 percent; the United States, 6.2 percent; France, 3.6 percent; the United Kingdom, 3.4 percent; Germany, 3.1 percent; and Italy, −0.01 percent. These income shares account for some of the differences in tax ratios in Table 1.

Another reason for this variation among countries is differences in provisions dealing with accelerated depreciation and investment tax credits. Some of these provisions are reported in Appendix A. In the case of very general measures, such as the immediate expensing of capital investments in the United Kingdom, there is little doubt that they will greatly reduce corporate tax liabilities and the relative importance of revenue raised from the corporate income tax. Provisions geared more specifically to promote investment in certain peripheral or depressed regions of a country probably have less effect, depending on the extent to which firms are induced to invest in activities that are less profitable. The Committee on Changing International Realities (CIR) study by Horst has calculated effects of these special tax measures on the corporate tax burden in five major OECD countries.[6] He judged that an allowance for general investment tax credits and accelerated depreciation schedules would result in effective corporate tax rates on domestic income as follows: Germany, 39.7 percent; the United States, 36.7 percent; France, 34.3 percent; Japan, 29.2 percent; and the United Kingdom, 17.8 percent.

That export earnings often are taxed less heavily than domestic income is also of importance in this analysis of international competitiveness. This may have little effect on the overall importance of corporate income taxes in a country, but it is highly relevant in assessing the international competitive impacts of fiscal intervention. Horst's estimates of the corporate tax burden on export earnings are as follows: Germany, 39.7 percent; the United States, 27.4 percent; Japan, 17.9 percent; the United Kingdom, 12.2 percent; and France, 8.7 percent. Further implications of these differences are discussed in the industry studies reported later in the report.

Neutrality in the Impacts of Different Taxes among Industries

In general, producers in a country that taxes them heavily are at a disadvantage competing in the same market with producers from a country that taxes them less. However, the national ratios of tax importance are a very generalized measure of tax impact; some taxes covered in Table 1 are levied on some industries or sectors and not on others and with variable impacts. But the most important revenues are derived from taxes that are universal (income taxes) or close to it (VAT on consumption but not saving). It is therefore of interest to consider whether these taxes are neutral, i.e., whether they affect all industries equally.

In the case of indirect taxes, imports and exports are treated differently from nontraded goods. Under present General Agreement on Tariffs and Trade (GATT) conventions, indirect taxes levied in the exporting country may be rebated at the border, and those applied in the importing country will be imposed when the good is brought into the country. This practice has been justified by the alleged neutrality of its effect on costs of imports versus competing domestic products. For instance, an increase in indirect taxes imposed equally on all goods will have no direct influence on the patterns of specialization or relative prices internationally that would exist in the absence of these taxes. The legality of such rebates, however, was at stake in the Zenith TV case mentioned in the "Introduction," and the sharp contrast between the importance of indirect taxes in the European countries and the United States (Table 1) suggests why this complaint has been raised by import-impacted industries in the United States. The U.S. argument implies rejection of the rationale for treating indirect taxes in such a way that no relative price effects would arise internationally, on the grounds that this same neutrality does not exist with direct taxes.

Concerning the neutrality of direct taxes, first consider the effects of a payroll tax. If labor-force participation is not responsive to changes in real wages received, then any tax on labor income in all industries will simply result in a corresponding decline in real wages with no change in relative commodity prices, regardless of whether a good requires a little or a lot of labor. That rationale would seem to lie behind the border-tax adjustment convention of the GATT, which provides that direct taxes are paid in the producing country and that no adjustments may be made when goods cross national boundaries. No adjustment need be made to prevent direct taxes from distorting relative prices and the comparative advantage that would exist without government intervention.

The key to this analysis of direct taxes was that the payroll tax could not be avoided and that labor-force participation was not responsive to the wages paid. In reality, not all payroll taxes are universal, but even if they were they could not cover leisure time. If aftertax real wages decline, some individuals may simply decide to work fewer hours, since they give up less by taking more leisure time. Higher payroll taxes would then result in reduced willingness to work, so that an increase in payroll taxes is likely to lead to some increase in beforetax wages to attract sufficient labor into the workforce. This higher labor cost will be reflected in the relative prices of goods produced within the economy, and thereby will affect international competitiveness.

With respect to taxes on capital, the corporate income tax clearly is not universal, since a significant noncorporate private sector exists in most countries. Thus, if corporate stockholders encounter an increase in the corporate income tax, it gives them an incentive to shift investment to the noncorporate sector. Returns to all capital will be driven down, and the price of output from the corporate sector will rise relative to that from the noncorporate sector since its cost of obtaining capital has increased. A further extension of this reasoning is to recognize that corporate shareholders may also have the option to invest in other countries, and they may be able to expand such investments without greatly reducing the foreign rate of return.

These comments suggest reasons why direct taxes may not be neutral in their effects on relative prices internationally, not merely in the short run but in the long run as well. The differences in tax incentives can result in differences in the national location of production as investors seek out their most profitable use of funds, and consequently different trade patterns result from the differences in tax practices.

SUBSIDIES

Subsidies are regarded here as government expenditure policies resulting in reduced production costs in a country. Therefore, to the extent that costs are reflected in prices charged, national subsidy policies can affect international competitiveness and the location of production internationally. Because direct expenditures often attract unwanted political attention, subsidy policies often do not appear as direct payments to producers for each unit of output sold. Rather, the awarding of loans, or the conditions of grants or government participation in an industry, may occur on terms that allow firms to raise capital more cheaply than they would without government intervention. Or certain government-sponsored training or research programs may allow firms to reduce their expenditures in these areas and utilize the technological discoveries. There is no easily defined list of policies that ought to be considered as forms of subsidy. The topics included here, for which some aggregate indicators can be constructed, are: direct operating subsidies, research and grants expenditures, and favorable financing of both domestic investment and export sales. Although not exhaustive, these categories capture a major part of most government fiscal intervention.

Operating Subsidies

Direct operating subsidies often are paid to government-run utilities, such as the postal service, rail transportation or electric power generation. These subsidies allow public enterprises to sell their output at prices that do not cover total costs, and these services may be inputs in the production of traded goods. Industries requiring large amounts of electric power, for instance, will be the greatest immediate beneficiaries of government subsidy policies to keep electricity prices low. Similarly, industries highly dependent on internal land transportation benefit from government policies to keep rail rates low.

Industries other than public utilities may receive direct government payments because their operations achieve certain social or political goals. One goal is guaranteeing employment in particular areas or sectors of the country. Some agricultural subsidies might fall in this category, as might the cost subsidies in shipbuilding and coal mining prevalent in many countries. Alternatively, some subsidies are provided because of the prestige or value for defense of maintaining a national producer in a particular industry. In other words, some governments seem to have adopted the goal of ensuring the survival of national producers in industries such as steel, chemicals, aircraft, computers, or automobiles.

Summing the direct operating subsidy payments within a country, and dividing by GDP, gives the figures reported in column one of Table 2. The larger values reported for France, Italy and the United Kingdom reflect the much larger role played by the public-sector enterprises in these economies than in Canada, Germany, Japan, or the United States. Examples are subsidies paid to large public holding companies in Italy; government assistance to coal mining and power production in France; and aid to railroads, British Steel and British Leyland in the United Kingdom. When firms can count on these direct subsidies to cover some portion of their costs, they need not raise

TABLE 2: AGGREGATE INDICATORS OF GOVERNMENT SUBSIDY POLICIES AS A PERCENTAGE OF GDP, 1976

	Current Account	Capital Formation, Gen'l. Gov't. and Public Enterprises	Capital Consumption, Gen'l. Gov't. and Public Enterprises	Aids to Private Capital Formation	Funds for R&D	Export Financing	
						Gov't. Supported Loans Outstanding	% of Exports Supported
Canada	1.7	4.9	2.1	0.9	0.6	0.7	4
France	2.7	5.2	2.0	0.6	1.0	0.5**	36
Germany	1.5	3.4*	1.0	0.3	0.9	0.3	10
Italy	2.6	10.5	2.7	1.1	n.a.	1.1	9
Japan	1.3	8.5	2.6	0.1	0.6	2.4	49
United Kingdom	2.8	8.6	4.3	0.9	1.1	2.1	36
United States	0.3	2.7	1.9	0.1	1.3	1.5	7

*Capital formation by public enterprises not reported.
**Includes only loans directly financed by the Banque Francaise en Commerce Exterieur.
n.a. = not available.

Sources:
Columns 1, 2 and 3: OECD, National Accounts, 1978.
Column 4: *Aid to Business in Canada*, p. 7; *Rapport sur les Comptes de la Nation de l'annee 1976*, vol. 3; *Subventionen, Problematik und Entwicklungen*, p. 57; "Special Intervention on Behalf of Southern Italy;" *National Income and Expenditure*; *The Budget of the United States Government*.
Column 5: Rachel McCulloch, *Research and Development as a Determinant of U.S. International Competitiveness* (Washington D.C.: NPA, 1978), p. 41.
Columns 6 and 7: Export-Import Bank of the United States, *Report to the U.S. Congress on Export Credit Competition and the Export-Import Bank of the United States*, March 1979.

prices or cut back output of unprofitable plants, and the location of production internationally is affected.[7]

Capital Subsidies

Capital transactions are also important as subsidy vehicles, both in the government provision of infrastructure such as sewage systems, transportation and communication networks, and with respect to the conditions under which capital financing is provided to private enterprises. The second and third columns of Table 2 give two different indications of public capital formation. Column two shows current investment by the government and public enterprises, while column three reports depreciation of the stock of such public capital. Comparing current public investment expenditures to current tax payments indicates their share in uses of the year's funds. The depreciation figures in column three give a better overall measure of the currently available benefits from government investment, although the funding had originated in past tax payments.[8] The fourth column shows government grants and loans for private investment; only data for current-year funding are available.

The limited role of government investment in the United States (columns two and three) can be attributed largely to the dominant role of private producers in utilities and transportation relative to the other countries. For countries such as Italy and Japan, where current investment (column two) is much larger than the current depreciation figure (column three), the numbers imply a more recently active role by the government in spurring public-sector capital formation. The very low value for the United States for aid to private investment (column four) again indicates a much smaller public role in investment.

The availability of government aid packages for industry has much more of an effect on location decisions among countries within Europe than the choice between locating there, in the United States or in Japan. An interesting dimension of European locational subsidy policies is the extent to which they are compatible with both EC goals and the separate growth and distribution targets of individual countries. In December 1978, the European Commission adopted new principles with respect to the coordination of regional aid, which were to be observed for the following three years.[9] The 1978 accord established for the first time a separate ceiling for employment subsidies, in addition to the previous limitations on the proportion of invested capital that could be provided through government aid. The effect of this modification was to increase the amount of aid that could be provided to labor-intensive industries. Allowable subsidies vary by the degree of development of the region where the investment is to be made. No limits at all are applied in the case of investment in Greenland! The most generous ceilings are those applied to Ireland, the Mezzogiorno of Italy, Northern Ireland, West Berlin, and the French Overseas Departments. Aid limits are set at 75 percent of initial investment cost, or 13,000 European Units of Account (1 EUA equalled $1.39 in October 1978) per job created. Other more developed areas qualify for less generous ceiling amounts of aid; but even in central, currently industrialized areas, grants are allowed up to 20 percent of investment cost of 3,500 EUA per job created. In general, the Commission does not appear to have adopted guidelines that would force major cutbacks in current programs.

It is important to remember that merely because grants are available does not mean that they are sufficiently attractive to lead to additional investment in a certain region or industry. Disadvantages such as poor communication facilities, high transportation costs either from input producers or to market centers, or an inadequately trained labor force may be sufficiently great to discourage much response to these incentives. The numerical approximations reported in column four of Table 2 give some measure of the extent to which government aids are both available and utilized.

Research and Development Subsidies

Closely related to investment grants are grants to support public and private research and development, shown in column five. McCulloch's CIR study supplies these estimates of government-funded research and development in 1973 as a percentage of gross domestic product.[10] Such funding should increase a country's ability to produce high technology goods, since the stock of technical know-how is expanded. In this area, the U.S. government appears to be intervening more than other governments do. To make a more accurate assessment of this situation, though, attention must be focused on the composition of this research. The greater importance of space and defense-related projects in the U.S. total may imply a smaller immediate commercial advantage than the raw figures suggest. Also, the relative rankings given here undoubtedly will change over time, as countries such as Japan carry out their stated goals of expanding government research support.[11]

Export Subsidies

The capital aid provisions discussed thus far are domestic policy measures that do not necessarily result in a price differential between home produced goods and those that are exported. Traditionally they have not been regarded as unfair favors or bounties to trade. Nevertheless, international competitiveness is affected since the effect of the aid is to lower the price of all production, thereby making imported goods less attractive while exported goods become more attractive. International agreements to control such domestic subsidies will be difficult to negotiate and implement. Symptomatic of this problem is the subsidy code tentatively agreed to in the Tokyo Round trade talks after extensive negotiations. Its effectiveness will remain uncertain until the actions of each signatory government demonstrate how they in fact will apply the code. Equally indicative of the difficulties that may be encountered is the lack of progress in controlling special financing conditions in the sale of exports. The scope of those special programs is indicated by the figures in columns six and seven of Table 2.

Column six gives the value of government-supported loans outstanding to finance exports, expressed as a percentage of GDP. These figures are fairly consistent with those reported in column seven, which gives the percentage of total exports from a country that benefits from some export support program. The figures suggest vigorous government intervention on the part of France, Japan and the United Kingdom, with a much smaller government role in Canada, Italy and the United States, where budget limitations exist or where lending agencies are not allowed to receive direct government subsidy. A further aspect of export promotion these figures do not capture is the trend toward mixed export credits. That term applies when foreign aid funds are used to allow concessionary interest rates to be offered to donor country exporters. The United States attempted to limit this practice, pursued by the French in particular, but only in October 1981 was an agreement reached to modify the 1976 International Arrangement on Officially Supported Export Credits.[12] Minimum lending rates of 10 percent to poor countries and 11 percent to rich countries were set, which both are below the 11.6 percent charged by the World Bank.

The lack of agreement in this area mirrors the conflicts that have arisen with respect to the taxation of export profits. That situation is exemplified by the EC's complaint lodged in 1973 against the U.S. Domestic International Sales Corporation provisions, which allowed U.S. exporters to defer taxation on a portion of their export profits. The United States raised a counter complaint before the GATT over the system of territorial taxation applied by France, Belgium and the Netherlands. In those countries, an exporter could avoid, and not simply defer, taxation on a large share of the profits. The GATT panels formed to consider these cases reported their judgment in 1976 that the systems applied in all four countries were inconsistent with the GATT articles of agreement. But because the European countries would not vote in favor of accepting these findings, GATT finally determined that the whole issue should be dropped.[13] Generally speaking, little effective action has been taken to curtail international competition in concessional export financing or tax concessions for export sales.

AGGREGATE FISCAL BALANCE

If taxes represent a burden on producers and subsidies and grants represent benefits, then balancing the positive and negative factors should yield a net indicator of the extent to which government fiscal intervention aids domestic producers. If the corporate income tax, for example, were treated as a factor that increased costs of production in a country by the same amount as the revenue it produced, while each dollar of direct operating or capital subsidy resulted in a corresponding reduction in private costs of production, the balance could provide an indicator of net benefits to the users of capital. While it is improbable that these precise conditions hold, international comparisons are still useful.

This indicator of net advantage is shown in column three of Table 3. The capital benefits calculation draws on the figures reported in Table 2 and includes the operating subsidy payments and the flow of services from the capital stock of public enterprises and the government. Because data regarding past investment loans and grants were not available, levels of these aids for a single year were included, rather than the sum of the annual saving in capital costs attributable to government assistance in previous years.[14]

If capital is mobile internationally and all other conditions are comparable, then capital would be expected to move to countries where the net balance of capital assistance is greater. Alternatively, if local conditions make investment in a country less favorable, the subsidy figures might be interpreted as showing the extent of fiscal intervention by the government to avoid an outflow of capital. These figures suggest that U.S. tax and subsidy policies result in relatively fewer fiscal incentives to attract or retain capital. If this approximate measure of fiscal intervention in the United States were to match levels of other countries, the likely outcome would be greater investment and production in the United States. Of course, these figures may change as a result of explicit changes in taxes and budgetary policy in the United States and elsewhere. Also, they will depend upon future inflation rates, which affect both the potential tax subsidy implicit in accelerated depreciation measures and the rate at which certain government expenditures grow.

The net balance indicator (column six of Table 3) rests on the following interpretation of the effects of tax and subsidy measures. In the rationale for neutrality of

TABLE 3: A GENERAL BALANCE OF TAX AND SUBSIDY POLICIES AS A PERCENTAGE OF GDP, 1976

	Subsidy-Tax Balance					
	Capital Elements			Capital & Labor Elements		
	Benefits	Taxes	Net	Benefits	Taxes	Net
Canada	5.4	3.8	1.6	28.4	32.9	−4.5
France	6.3	2.3	4.0	37.0	39.5	−2.5
Germany	3.7	1.7	2.0	33.0	36.7	−3.7
Italy	6.5	2.2	4.3	35.7	35.8	−0.1
Japan	4.9	3.5	1.4	21.9	20.9	+1.0
United Kingdom	9.3	1.7	7.6	34.6	36.7	−2.1
United States	3.8	3.0	0.8	23.4	29.3	−5.9

Sources: Column 1: Table 2, sum of columns 1, 3, 4, and 5 and 10 percent of column 6.
Column 2: Table 1, column 5.
Column 3: Column 1 minus column 2.
Column 4: OECD, *National Accounts*; government nondefense spending, social security benefits, unfunded employee benefits, and Table 2, columns 1 and 3.
Column 5: Table 1, column 1.
Column 6: Column 4 minus column 5.

direct taxes, described earlier, an implicit assumption is that taxes on labor income cannot be avoided; but recent labor-market research suggests the opposite, that labor-force participation is sensitive to real wages earned.[15] Where labor does withdraw from the labor force when real wages fall, then taxes that reduce the real value of wages would have to be offset by corresponding benefits of government expenditures and transfers in order that labor-force participation remain unchanged. Only then will a country's relative labor costs be unaffected. A broad range of taxes affect the real value of income and thereby fall in this category—not just payroll taxes but also sales and income taxes.

Column six of Table 3 reflects this assumed situation, comparing the total tax burden in a country versus the benefits from government expenditures. The benefit measure leaves out spending for national defense and also for transfer programs under which benefits are quite unrelated to contributions. In other words, if taxpayers fund projects that yield benefits primarily to nontaxpayers, workers are more likely to regard their tax payment as reducing real wages. Conversely, if social security taxes fund health and pension benefits that are more directly related to an employee's contribution, those taxes are less likely to be regarded as reducing real wages. The figures in column four of Table 3, then, partially reflect the extent to which the government pursues goals other than national defense and income redistribution; the more important those two goals, the smaller the direct benefit figure will be. The net benefit results reported in column six again suggest that government fiscal intervention in the United States has the greatest likelihood of resulting in higher production costs, with respect to the use of both capital and labor. Employment in the United States is discouraged and foreign relative to domestic investment is encouraged.

The measures reported in columns three and six at best represent approximations that suggest directions in which production patterns would be affected internationally due to government fiscal intervention. In actuality, any economy involves the production of thousands of goods, and government policies seldom have precisely proportional impact on each industry. As some industries expand and others contract, resources are transferred out of some sectors and into others. The resources required in the expanding sectors will differ from those released by the contracting sectors. Returns to capital and labor in given sectors may change over time, which further affects how much different sectors may be impacted. This recognition that tax and subsidy policies generally have different effects across industries is what motivates the more detailed industry studies presented in Chapter 3.

Notes

1   Arthur Andersen & Co., *Pocket Guide to European Corporate Taxes, Third Edition* (1975). The year 1976 is used in all comparisons of tax and budgetary policy. Although more recent data are available with respect to some of the information reported, government subsidy measures cannot be updated very easily. In order to approximate the combined effects of fiscal intervention in all the countries studied, 1976 became the base year.

2   Organization for Economic Cooperation and Development, *The 1978 Tax/Benefit Position of a Typical Worker in OECD Member Countries* (Paris, 1979).

3   Ibid.

4   See country summaries by Price Waterhouse, Arthur Andersen and Ernst & Ernst. The U.S. corporate income tax rate on earnings greater than $100,000 became 46 percent, effective in taxable years beginning after December 31, 1978.

5   A distinction should be made between countries that have integrated personal and corporate income tax systems and those that have not. In the former, a portion of corporate tax payments may be claimed as tax credits by stockholders who receive corporate dividends. An assessment of the effect of the corporate income tax on capital costs would be misleading if it were based on the statutory rate or gross corporate tax payment in countries that integrated tax systems. For a U.S. subsidiary operating in these countries, dividends paid to the parent do not lead to any corresponding reduction in tax liability as they would for a resident of the country; in the United Kingdom, this situation is partially addressed in the new United Kingdom-United States Tax Treaty.

6   Thomas Horst, *Income Taxation and Competitiveness in the United States, West Germany, France, the United Kingdom, and Japan* (Washington, D.C.: NPA, 1977), p. 20.

7   Again, effects comparable to these explicit subsidies may arise due to government regulations. For instance, price controls imposed on oil and natural gas in Canada and the United States benefit industries that require relatively more of those inputs. On the other hand, U.S. requirements that domestic flag ships be used in intracoastal navigation impose higher costs on industries which rely on that form of transportation.

8   Some public capital formation is financed by user fees, such as charges for postal and telecommunication services or for utilities. The more important these forms of public investment are relative to those that provide services for which no user fees are charged then the greater the possible overstatement of fiscal subsidy implicit in these figures. Unfortunately, disaggregated data were not available to use in pursuing this qualification.

9   For an account of the various standards adopted, see Commission of the European Communities, *Eighth Report on Competition Policy* (Brussels, 1979), pp. 109-112.

10   Rachel McCulloch, *Research and Development as a Determinant of U.S. International Competitiveness* (Washington, D.C.: NPA, 1978), p. 41.

11   Economic Planning Agency, *New Economic and Social Seven-Year Plan* (Tokyo: Foreign Press Center, 1979), p. 43.

12   "Japanese Approval Clinches Agreement on New Interest Rates for Export Credits," *Wall Street Journal*, October 22, 1981.

13   For a summary of this situation see U.S. Department of the Treasury, *The Operation and Effect of the Domestic International Sales Corporation Legislation, 1977 Annual Report* (Washington, D.C., 1978), pp. 10-17.

14   For an example of how this cost saving calculation might be made, paying attention to the breakdown of additional investment into structures and equipment and applying the appropriate depreciation rate to each, see G. Denton, S. O'Cleireacain and S. Ash, *Trade Effects of Public Subsidies to Private Enterprises* (London: MacMillan, 1975), pp. 282-283. This discussion also raises a more fundamental methodological issue. Suppose that a grant is used to buy a capital asset. After that asset is fully depreciated, has the subsidy effect of the grant been exhausted or should allowance be made for the possible re-investment of earnings generated from the grant? The present procedure ignores this potential re-investment and thereby reflects a single snapshot that likely understates the importance of past policies. This qualification seems particularly important in the case of Japan, as discussed in the industry studies of Chapter 3.

15   Glen Cain and Harold Watts, *Income Maintenance and Labor Supply* (Chicago: Rand McNally, 1973); Daniel Hammermesh, "New Estimates of the Incidence of the Payroll Tax," *Southern Economic Journal,* Vol. 45, No. 4 (April 1979), pp. 1208-1219.

Industry Studies 3

Any interpretation of the aggregate measures discussed thus far implicitly rests on the assumption that all industries within a country experience the same proportional harm or benefit from tax and subsidy policies. For instance, if national output is encouraged by government fiscal intervention and foreign capital flows into the country to take advantage of the situation, then all industries are assumed to benefit equally from this inflow. In reality, government policies are likely to have disproportionate effects on industries within an economy, often as a direct goal of government policy. The purpose of this chapter is to evaluate the international competitive effects of policies that reflect direct government interest in promoting the production of five specific industries: textiles, steel, automobiles, pharmaceuticals, and computers. Direct grants, government equity participation, favorable loan conditions, and special depreciation allowances accorded to a particular industry are examples of the policies to be considered. More general factors, such as a high corporate tax burden that would affect all capital-intensive corporate producers, are not dealt with because these disincentives are broader than the industry-specific policies to be examined. Also, this portion of the study focuses on the impact effects of industry-specific policies without tracing out the many possible repercussions within the economy, as relative prices, wages rates and returns to capital change after the initial impact of a policy is felt. A particular drawback of ignoring these additional adjustments is that one too easily can lose sight of the fact that all industries will not expand at the same time as a result of government intervention. Rather, if government policies favor particular industries, and if they are to expand, then resources generally must be bid away from other industries receiving no explicit subsidy. Thus, a portion of any subsidy or tax break given to a particular industry merely offsets the advantage given to other industries through other types of tax and subsidy programs.

The reason for not pursuing those repercussions here is that little attention previously has been paid even to the impact effects of government intervention. While economists can evaluate how tax and subsidy policies affect the cost of capital to a single producer in a fairly straightforward manner, there are several ways in which that cost reduction may affect competitiveness internationally, if it does so at all. For example, the cost saving may result in a lower price charged per unit of output, higher labor compensation, a greater amount of R&D expenditure, an expanded sales force and greater advertising, diversification into other industries, or a higher dividend payout to stockholders. Which of these alternative outcomes occurs depends on a variety of different circumstances, such as the extent of product differentiation, and the degree of industry concentration. As a consequence, no single model appropriately can be applied to all of the industries studied.

One possible approach is to assume that a competitive market exists for a fairly standardized product. In that case, the effect of more favorable government tax and subsidy policies most likely will be to allow a lower price to be charged internationally. That approach will be followed in the case of the steel industry. Two major competitive effects are captured by the model explained in Appendix B. One is the extent to which a subsidy allows the producing country to reduce its price and expand exports. The other is the way in which a subsidy reduces that country's dependence on imports, thereby resulting in the deflection of those goods to other markets. The estimates reported here will focus on the combination of these impacts felt by U.S. producers as a result of foreign tax and subsidy practices.

In other industries, products may be quite differentiated, possibly the result of past expenditures on research and product development. In those cases only a small percentage of the price charged in the market may reflect physical input costs, while the remainder reflects a return to knowledge. Consequently, any tax and subsidy measures are less likely to affect market prices of currently produced goods than the discovery and introduction of new products. This possibility of competition through innovation seems most appropriate in the case of industries such as pharmaceuticals and computers. Past analyses of the innovation process in these two industries will be examined in projecting the competitive effects of policies that make available more funds for research and product development. A further issue considered is where such funds may be spent and where the subsequent income flow is earned. Both of these questions are quite relevant in high technology industries where the global operations of multinational corporations play a dominant role.

Whatever the approach adopted, the implication should not be drawn that tax and subsidy policies are the sole determinant of international competitiveness or that a complete picture of relative competitive positions has been presented. Tax and subsidy policies may be widespread, but their competitive effects largely may be negated through quantitative trade restrictions, as in the case of textiles. Alternatively, restrictions on foreign investment and production, or regulation over the introduction of new products, may be more important determinants of international competitiveness than the factors focused on here. These additional issues are discussed where they appear to be of particular relevance in each industry study.

Even when the relevant competitive effects can be determined, interpreting the projected changes in output is not straightforward. An estimated reduction in industry output of one-half of one percent will be referred to as relatively small in this study. This is not to say that such displacements will be spread evenly throughout the nation to avoid significant impacts in particular communities. Rather, the projected effects are considered small relative to the output changes resulting from other factors such as trade policies, technological improvements or environmental controls.

THE TEXTILE INDUSTRY

In practically all of the countries studied, the textile industry has been characterized by rather stagnant or even declining employment. These results for the industry as a whole mask even more severe problems faced by particular groups within the industry. The social and economic problems created by industry contraction often are compounded in the developed countries by the regional concentration of textile output in areas where few alternative employment opportunities exist.

The extent to which tax and subsidy policies have played an important role in bolstering this industry varies across countries. In general, the role of tax incentives has been limited, since tax forgiveness is an effective incentive only if positive profits are being earned and substantial tax otherwise would have been paid. Grants have played a role in the rationalization programs of some countries, but they have not been a major determinant of international competitiveness. Rather, voluntary export restraints negotiated under the Multifiber Arrangement (MFA) have been a more important determinant of the amount of adjustment necessary in each country.[1] A successor to the Long-Term Cotton Textile Arrangement first adopted in 1961, the MFA became effective in 1974 and was later renewed for another four years in December 1977. The MFA essentially represents a compromise, intended to avoid sudden surges in imports that cause major domestic market disruptions, but at the same time designed to allow imports to grow at an orderly rate (6 percent annually). In 1977, MFA agreements covered 76 percent of U.S. textile imports, which gives an indication of the ability to control imports but which also suggests some of the uncertainty possible. The way in which each country negotiates its own set of bilateral export restraints, and the claims it makes for exceptions to the general expectation of import market growth, directly affect imports. Precise control over MFA imports does not exist, though, because most bilateral agreements allow a certain portion of the quota to be carried forward or backward from one year to another. Because the actual level of imports is an important determinant of domestic adjustments required, attention must be paid to the trade policy pursued. The trade and aid policies adopted reflect the government's judgment of how large a textile industry should be preserved in the long run and how fast the domestic industry should be forced to adjust to this target.

The Canadian case is considered first.[2] In 1970, a Canadian Textile Policy was established and a Textile and Clothing Board was formed. The board's primary function has been to investigate complaints of market disruption and to determine appropriate remedies. Unlike the directives given to comparable groups in other countries, an important consideration in judgments by the Canadian TCB is to be the long-run viability of the industry without additional quota protection, i.e., if only the current tariff were enforced. This viewpoint presumably represents a less protectionist stance, which also is reflected in the limitation of import restrictions to specific product categories that compete most directly with Canadian output. Also, Canadian producers petitioning to receive relief from foreign dumping must prove that price discrimination between home and foreign markets actually is occurring, not merely that sales are being made at less than average total cost.

Taken together, these separate policy actions suggest that the Canadian textile industry has been forced to make substantial adjustments to increased foreign competition. Within Canada, production is concentrated geographically in Ontario and Quebec, and employment in textiles and apparel account for roughly 20 percent of industrial employment in Quebec. Therefore, textile policy has definite regional implications.

Government subsidy programs do exist to aid displaced workers and to help finance investment in more efficient capital equipment. The General Adjustment Assistance Program provides direct loans or government guarantees of private loans. Forty percent of all loans outstanding from this fund had been granted to the textile industry in 1974. Additionally, the Department of Regional Economic Expansion makes grants of up to 20 percent of the capital cost in plant modernizations, and up to 15 percent of the cost of new facilities, plus $5,000 per job created. Many textile producers are located in depressed regions where investment would qualify for such grants.

Despite these aid programs, employment has declined, as shown in Table 4. In November 1976, Canada invoked the GATT safeguard clause (Article XIX) and imposed global quotas on several textile products. Then, under the second MFA, Canada was

TABLE 4: COMPARATIVE TEXTILE INDUSTRY STATISTICS (SITC 65)

	Real Production (1970=100)	Employment (1970=100)	Import Values			Export Values		
			1977 U.S.$ Millions	% of Consumption	Relative to 1970	1977 U.S.$ Millions	% of Shipments	Relative to 1970
Canada	109.4*	89*	$ 995	23.1	1.41	$ 144	4.2	1.03
France	107.3	96	2,368	26.1	2.80	2,240	23.6	1.61
Germany	105.8	67	4,171	28.2	1.95	4,103	27.8	1.83
Italy	104.2*	85*	1,333	17.0	2.08	2,476	25.1	1.90
Japan	99.8	60	0.866	50.0	2.58	3,712	81.1	1.42
United Kingdom	92.4	73	1,951	19.7	2.11	2,003	20.0	1.40
United States	122.6	94	1,790	4.4	1.05	1,959	4.8	2.16

*Data for 1975.
Relative changes in imports and exports deflated by U.S. textile output deflator.
Sources: OECD, *Textile Industry in OECD Countries*, various issues; U.N., *Yearbook of Industrial Statistics*, various issues; and OECD, *Trade by Commodities*, various issues.

able to negotiate a larger number of bilateral agreements than previously, which cut import growth rates well below the target rate of 6 percent and severely limited substitution between sensitive product categories.[3] This greater reliance on trade policy is mirrored in the experiences of several other countries, too.

The decline of the textile industry in the United Kingdom has occurred over several decades. A review of the various strategies adopted over the postwar period is particularly instructive.[4] The Cotton Industry Act of 1959 was designed to eliminate excess capacity and to encourage modernization of the domestic textile industry. The aim was to scrap 50 percent of spinning capacity and 40 percent of weaving capacity. Payments to firms scrapping equipment were made on the basis of a fixed rate per machine, with an additional premium if the firm were to cease operations entirely. Financing of these payments was obtained from the government (two-thirds share) and from those firms remaining in the industry (one-third share). Total expenditures under the program amounted to $70 million, and a fair amount of old, and conceivably worthless, equipment was scrapped. Consequently, the program did inject government funds to improve the cash flow of some firms in the industry, but by levying part of the cost on those remaining in the industries, the net impact on British competitiveness becomes smaller than under an operating subsidy paid to whatever firm found it efficient to expand output.

The experiment with making compensatory payments to those scrapping equipment was not repeated in later policies directed at the textile industry as a whole. Perhaps this was due to the belief that compensation was being paid for steps that private firms should have carried out in their own self-interest. However, plans adopted in the 1970s for rationalization of wool textile production limited modernization financing to those companies that scrapped old plant.[5] Projects combining rebuilding and re-equipment could qualify for a 20 percent subsidy, but to assure that total productive capacity was not increased, recipients were required to scrap an equal amount of existing capacity in the case of combining machines, and an amount equal to 90 percent of new capacity in the case of cards, spindles, looms, and dying facilities. For plant closings, payments of 4 percent of the sales of the last year of operation would be made, or a scale of payments according to the type of equipment scrapped could be chosen. Total appropriations for the program were $36 million.

Current aids are not geared specifically to the industry, but are available through regional development grants, cited previously. Trade policies have played an increasingly important role, particularly after Great Britian's entry into the Common Market. Pressure for restrictionist policies rose through the 1970s, as might be expected from the figures recorded in Table 4, which show a decline in employment of 27 percent over the period 1970-77, and an actual decline in the volume of output, too. This experience, part of it occurring under the initial MFA that ran from 1974 to 1977, led the United Kingdom, together with France, to oppose extension of the MFA unless the basic agreement was changed or more stringent bilateral export restraints were negotiated. The push for greater protection can be expected to continue in the future, but even new agreements are unlikely to be so restrictive as to stabilize employment at current levels.

The Japanese experience is not one of continued decline over the entire postwar period, as in the case of Britain, but efforts to deal with inefficient production facilities have led to scrapping policies within Japan. Although Japan still is a major world exporter of textiles, Japanese economic plans reported by the Ministry of International Trade and Industry (MITI) project much slower growth of output in this sector, continued adjustment toward greater capital intensity and further contraction of employment.[6] In particular, employment in textiles fell 32 percent from 1970 through 1975 and is projected to decline another 12 percent by 1985. Output is projected to grow at an annual rate of 1.9 percent through 1985. MITI plans call for the scrapping of 20 to 30 percent of capacity and reorganization through vertical integration within the industry.

How are these reductions to be encouraged, and what measures are available to lessen the adjustment impact? Medium-size and small spinning enterprises that abandoned target numbers of spindles were eligible to receive, interest-free, 16-year loans.[7] Also, interest rates on loans outstanding from government banking institutions were to be reduced to a maximum of 8.9 percent (8.6 percent in the case of medium and small enterprises).

With respect to all impacted industries, under a new law adopted in May 1978, measures are to be taken through the Relief of Structurally Depressed Industries Act. Some of the first groups to be designated as depressed were four different synthetic fiber producers. A Depressed Industries Credit Fund has been established, which has the initial capital to guarantee nearly 100 billion yen in adjustment loans. Tax provisions to benefit those firms shifting into new lines of business were proposed in 1978, to permit additional first-year depreciation allowances to be claimed for three years, a measure projected to offer potential benefits to producers of 200 to 300 billion yen. Furthermore, the Labor Ministry has responsibility for the operation of the Employment Stabilization Fund, which can provide subsidies to structurally depressed enterprises. Founded in October 1977, it is funded by employment insurance contributions. Sixteen textile and clothing industries are eligible for such assistance. These subsidies amount to payments of one-half of the allowances (three-fourths in the case of small enterprises) given by firms to workers placed on paid leave, a status where they usually receive two-thirds or more of full-time wages. However, the payments were to be made for a maximum of 75 days, and a firm had to release 25 percent of its workforce (20 percent for small enterprises) to be eligible. These restrictions resulted in very little initial usage of the plan, and consequently the workforce reductions to establish eligibility were reduced to 12.5 percent (10 percent in small enterprises) in October 1978.

The trade figures reported in Table 4 show that the growth of imports has been much more rapid than the growth of exports. Aside from the greater competition of low wage producers, the slower growth of exports may be attributable in part to two additional factors, the appreciation of the Japanese yen and also the elimination in 1972 of special accelerated depreciation measures that could be claimed in accord with a firm's growth in export earnings.[8] This shift in the textile trade balance undoubtedly will continue as resources are moved out of an industry where Japan's comparative advantage is fast disappearing. Japanese textile producers have been pushing for stricter import controls and have indicated, just as producers in many other countries, that loan guarantees are of little use if the market progressively will be dominated by imports from low wage countries.

With respect to the European countries, reference already has been made to the British experience, much of which covered the period before the United Kingdom joined the European Community. Actually, cooperative European action has been fairly recent. In 1971, the EC established a framework to coordinate the diverse national aid plans designed to benefit the textile industry and particularly to prevent major escalation in such programs without consideration being given to overall capacity requirements in the industry within the EC.[9] Basic principles were to prohibit aid designed merely to keep firms in business or to expand total capacity. Rather, aid was to be geared to activities such as R&D expenditure, the elimination of excess productive capacity or the conversion to production of other goods.

Although Italy is a net exporter of textiles, employment in the industry is falling. An Italian plan to aid textile producers through a 10-year income tax exemption was mentioned previously as an example of the type of program prohibited by the European Commission. Subsequent Italian plans have run afoul of the Commission, too.[10] One such proposal was to introduce a 3-year reduction in the family allowance tax paid by firms in the textile and garment industries, from 15 percent to 10 percent. That measure was estimated to provide tax relief of approximately 31 billion lira, or roughly 0.8 percent of turnover. The Commission ruled against this proposal in 1973 because it did not involve a restructuring element, but rather appeared to be an imprecisely targeted policy that would merely maintain inefficient producers. The Italian government appealed this decision to the Court of Justice, which dismissed the case in 1974 on the grounds that focusing on this single tax element, which admittedly contributed to relatively higher costs in textiles as compared to other industries, was inappropriate. In a 1975 case, objections were raised to an Italian proposal that would have made grants available to medium-size producers to enable them to take over some insolvent companies. The plan was approved only after modifications were made to limit sharply the amount of new capacity created.

With respect to other European producers, the German trade balance in textiles has not deteriorated as much as the French. Yet, the reduction in German employment over the period from 1970 through 1977 was particularly sharp, whereas French employment seemed to stabilize. German fiscal assistance measures have been fairly limited. Also, within the EC, Germany has taken a less protectionist stance than France and Britain. Nevertheless, Neu calculated that a tariff giving protection equivalent to that from the level of quotas in 1974 would have been 45 percent.[11] To the extent that layoffs in Germany have been concentrated among foreign guest workers, this factor probably has blunted some of the political pressure for even more protectionist policies. On the other hand, France unilaterally introduced restrictions in June 1977 and removed them only after the EC adopted emergency restrictions to be in effect until the new MFA was negotiated.[12] The EC forced a major change in the nature of the MFA by ignoring any obligation to demonstrate on a case by case basis why exceptions to the 6 percent growth target should be allowed. New bilateral agreements sharply reduced imports of sensitive products below 1976 levels, and annual growth rates were set at levels such as 0.28 percent for cotton yarn and 0.5 percent for cotton woven fabrics. However, while these more stringent requirements have been imposed on sales by the successful Asian producers, the overall slowdown of imports has not been as severe due to the relatively large role of sales from former colonies and European Free Trade Area countries.

A compounding factor in the European situation has been the growth in U.S. textile exports, which are not controlled by the MFA. In 1979, the U.S share of the chemical fiber market in Italy and in the United Kingdom jumped from well under 10 percent to over 25 percent. Europeans complained that U.S. producers received an advantage, due to cheaper input costs made possible by controlled petroleum and natural gas prices in the United States. In September 1980, the European Commission levied antidumping duties against U.S exporters of polyester yarns, and a broader investigation of U.S. polyester fabric exports was initiated.[13] Independently, the United Kingdom imposed quotas against U.S. exports of nylon and polyester yarns. Broader steps covering other man-made fibers were under consideration in 1981.

Given the recent growth in U.S. exports, it is not surprising that the U.S. textile industry has not been forced to contract as severely as producers in other developed countries. If the U.S. position as a net exporter in fact does depend upon the input cost advantage cited above, then this position likely will be reversed with the decontrol of U.S. petroleum prices in 1981. If, instead, the U.S. position is due to changes in other cost relationships, particularly the depreciation of the dollar since 1970, then a sharp fall in exports is unlikely.

The current favorable position of U.S. textile producers also is indicated by the extent to which quotas negotiated under the MFA are not being filled. Regarding the top three suppliers to the United States in 1978, Hong Kong filled 99.6 percent of its quota for apparel made of cotton and man-made fibers, but only 64.5 percent of its quota for fabrics and yarns made of cotton and man-made fibers; the corresponding figures for Korea were 82.0 percent and 88.4 percent, and for Taiwan 93.0 percent and 66.8 percent.[14]

Direct aid to U.S. textile producers has been made available under the Trade Act of 1974. Through September 1979, trade adjustment assistance (TAA) payments of $22 million had been made to 18,450 displaced textile workers, and low interest loans of roughly $8 million had been granted to 23 textile firms whose sales had declined and who were unable to obtain private financing. Compared to industry output of $40 billion in 1977 alone, these aid figures are quite small. Aid to the more labor-intensive apparel industry has been on a larger scale, with over 97,000 workers and 148 firms certified to receive TAA benefits through September 1979.[15]

By way of summary, the textile industry has faced serious import competition from low wage countries, although the market shift toward man-made fibers has reduced some of the advantage of these countries. Attempts to aid the textile industry through tax incentives, grants and loans have been fairly specifically targeted to firms feeling the most impact and have not been made generally available to all firms in the industry. Also, most aids have the stated intent of encouraging restructuring and re-equipment without expanding overall capacity, although regional development grants may not carry these same restrictions. A major policy objective would appear to be slowing down the rate at which domestic industries must adjust to declining employment prospects, but this goal has been addressed primarily through trade policies that limit the amount of foreign competition faced, both from nations covered by MFA agreements and those free from current quota limitations. Direct subsidy and aid packages have been too small to affect greatly domestic prices or output and instead have had their greatest effect in keeping the weakest firms from making all of the adjustment.

THE STEEL INDUSTRY

Over the decade of the '70s, a majority of the countries studied experienced declining output and employment in their domestic steel industries. That situation is reflected in the figures through 1977 presented in Table 5, and the cyclical downturn in 1980 further accentuated that trend. Because the steel industry is a major source of employment, governments have taken an active role to affect the rate of decline that occurs. No comprehensive agreement has been negotiated to regulate international trade in steel in a manner similar to the MFA concerning textiles, but individual countries increasingly have turned to trade policy measures to supplement other industry aid packages. Government ownership has been an important factor among the various types of aid provided, although it carries with it the liability that regional development

**TABLE 5: COMPARATIVE STEEL INDUSTRY STATISTICS, 1977
(SITC 67, Excluding 671)**

	Crude Steel Production (1970 = 100)	Employment (1970 = 100)	Imports (1970 = 100)	Import Share of Consumption	Exports (1970 = 100)	Export Share of Shipments
Canada	1.21	1.14[a]	1.0	0.13	1.3	0.13
France	0.93	1.03	1.3	0.39	1.5	0.44
Germany	0.87	0.90	1.6	0.42	1.3	0.40
Italy	1.35	1.31	0.8	0.21	3.9	0.29
Japan	1.10	0.91	*	*	1.9	0.33
United Kingdom	0.73	0.60	2.4	0.20	1.1	0.22
United States	0.95	0.86	1.7	0.18	0.3	0.02

[a]1975.
*Negligible.
Source: OECD, *Steel Industry in OECD Countries*, various issues, and U.N. Economic Commission for Europe, *Statistics of World Trade in Steel*, various issues.

goals or price control measures sought by the government can be imposed more directly on government-owned enterprises.

The U.S. Federal Trade Commission (FTC) released a study in 1977 that catalogued and assessed many of these provisions.[16] Estimates of the scope of recent government assistance efforts favoring the steel industry were made for a variety of countries. Subjective evaluations also were made of the extent to which regional aid packages merely offset the disadvantages of locating in depressed regions or provided incentives that would lead to an expansion of output beyond what otherwise would have been constructed anywhere in the country. The FTC concluded that government aids at most amounted to 1 percent of total production costs, with the exception of Britain, and consequently had little effect on international patterns of trade. The purpose of this review is to consider whether more recent measures have altered this judgment of a minimal cost effect and to assess whether even a larger cost impact would yield large competitive effects internationally.

The leading role of the Japanese in world steel markets is commonly acknowledged. Yet, the Japanese government already has announced the goal of shifting away from industries that require considerable energy and raw material inputs. MITI's long-range projections through 1985 call for slower growth in the steel industry than for the economy as a whole and an annual rate of decline in employment of 0.6 percent.[17] This situation contrasts markedly with the very rapid build up in the 1950s and '60s; even over the period 1965–75, output was growing at nearly 20 percent annually.

Government assistance was much more important in the 1950s and '60s, when output rapidly expanded, than it is now. After World War II, the steel industry was designated an important industry to be promoted by government action, first through the subsidization of input prices and then in the 1950s through direct loans.[18] Although the importance of government loans declined in the late 1950s and '60s, the priority the industry was accorded by the government undoubtedly led to easier access to private financing. Also, special depreciation allowances that permitted larger initial write offs of up to 50 percent of capital invested were made available to important industries in the early 1950s and phased out only in 1976. Pechman and Kaizuka report that in 1970, for example, these special depreciation measures, plus the accelerated depreciation provisions tied to export sales, accounted for 22 percent of all depreciation claimed by the steel industry.[19] This figure is significantly higher than for most other industries, and Pechman and Kaizuka cite the judgment that these special provisions had their major sectoral impact in promoting the steel and machinery industries. The willingness to use the tax system to promote particular industries appears greater than in the United States or most European countries, not too surprising a result given the minimal role that outright grants have played. Finally, the large initial write offs currently available on investments to meet pollution standards might be considered favorable to the steel industry, although Japanese pollution abatement expenditures in steel have been greater than in the United States.[20]

More currently, MITI plans called for the scrapping of three million tons of excess capacity of open hearth and electric furnace facilities in 1978.[21] Because most of these installations are obsolete, the change contemplated in Japan's international trading position is not great. Small-scale producers in these segments of the steel industry have been designated structurally depressed and have been eligible to receive both interest rate reductions on outstanding loans and labor subsidies from the Employment Stabilization Fund, as already discussed with respect to the adjustment of the textile industry. One possibility encouraging the scrapping of facilities would be to adopt a system of direct payments to producers who reduce output, such as adopted in the aluminum industry. In that case, the level of compensation is calculated at the annual rate of 6.6 percent of the book value of frozen facilities.[22]

In summary, while the government played an active role in the growth and promotion of the steel industry, a study commissioned by the American Iron and Steel Institute concludes that "it is difficult to ascribe a significant cost advantage to Japanese producers resulting from incentives or subsidies."[23]

With respect to the other countries studied, Table 5 reflects the net export position of Europe as a whole. Yet, steel industry output has fallen since 1976, and European analysts have projected that 1974's peak production will not be achieved again until 1985. The general recessionary conditions in the steel industry have led to expanded EC involvement in the rationalization of the industry. Loans under provisions of the European Coal and Steel Community more than tripled from 1976 to 1978, reaching a level of roughly $280 million in the latter year.[24] The ECSC has been able to borrow funds successfully due to its ability to assess a levy of up to 1 percent on the value of members' sales. This ability to borrow as a group is particularly significant as individual private enterprises incurring large losses have much less access to private capital markets. European Investment Bank loans also have been an important source of funds in aiding the steel industry, particularly in 1976 and 1977 when substantial loans were made to producers in the United Kingdom and Italy. Some of the loans have been made at interest rates 3 percent below the formula rate linked to current money market conditions.

Also in 1978, compulsory minimum prices were established on many steel products, to be applied to trade within the EC.[25] These prices were established simultaneously with a set of temporary reference prices imposed on foreign imports. More importantly from the international standpoint, agreements were reached with the 15 foreign countries that are the EC's major sources of imported steel; the agreements had the aim of limiting imports and of preserving trade patterns as they existed in 1976. This battery of loan and trade measures adopted by the EC demonstrates that depressed conditions in the steel industry were much more general than in the United States alone. This EC response is presented at the outset primarily because its common external trade policy generally rules out individual policy initiatives by member countries. Considerable scope for government action still exists with respect to national adjustment measures to aid the steel industry, and these individual policies are considered next.

To analyze the U.K. situation is essentially to analyze the operation of the British Steel Corporation (BSC).[26] Nationalization of the steel industry occurred in 1950, but a new Conservative government embarked on a denationalization program in 1951. Government control over pricing and investment decisions continued in the 1950s and '60s, and general uncertainty over possible renationalization of the industry undoubtedly also contributed to its poor performance. That renationalization took place in 1967. Since then, government goals with respect to regional output and employment, as well as the tone of labor relations, have represented external constraints on BSC's operations. Correspondingly, considerable government aid has been provided to BSC.

One of the most significant subsidy aspects of public ownership is that few dividends are ever paid to the government as a shareholder. The 1967 nationalization plan called for BSC to assume a debt of $3 billion, which included compensation to shareholders of the acquired firms and assumption of their outstanding debts. These debt-service payments could not be met, and the FTC report indicates that consequently $1.7 billion of the total was converted into public dividend capital, on which interest no longer was due (but dividends were to be paid out of expected profits). Further financial problems in 1971 led to a writing down of both the remaining interest-bearing debt and the amount of public dividend capital on which dividends were to be paid.

Since then, considerable aid has continued to flow to BSC. The actual amount of financial assistance has varied year by year, but a few figures can usefully summarize the situation. In March 1979, long-term indebtedness was £1,549.2 million ($3.2 billion), roughly one-half of which was owed to the Secretary of State for Industry.[27] Another major portion was owed to foreign creditors, with full repayment guaranteed by the British government. With respect to the state loans, the March 1978 interest rate charged was 10 percent, clearly below the interest rate of 12.5 percent paid by the government on its own long-term bonds. Thus, a very conservative estimate of the subsidy element implicit in these loans would be £20 million ($41 million). Regional development grants accounted for £400 million ($814 million) of capital employed. The annual subsidy element of such grants would be approximately £60 million ($122 million). Finally, public dividend capital amounted to £1,824 million ($3.7 billion), and a new subscription of government capital in 1979 amounted to £850 million ($1.7 billion). Since no dividends were paid on either of these two categories of capital, an implicit subsidy of £400 million ($814 million) arises here, assuming a 15 percent return to equity. Therefore, the total subsidy elements identified here are £480 million, or 14.5 percent of sales.

The rates of decline of both employment and output reported in Table 5 indicate that in proportional terms the U.K. steel industry has faced the greatest adjustment of any of the countries studied. Further contraction has taken place since 1977. BSC annual reports cite a fall in output of 9 percent and a drop in employment of 10.5 percent from fiscal year 1977 to 1979. Not surprisingly, the government has felt compelled to cushion this adjustment. The fact that this aid has influenced international trade patterns seems equally as clear, since subsidies have maintained jobs and productive capacity that otherwise would have been eliminated. U.K. exports would have been smaller and imports larger. For example, U.S. Treasury data indicate that in 1977 BSC was underpricing Japanese steel companies on the west coast of the United States,[28] a situation that would seem to signal a political decision to cover BSC losses in order that they maintain employment. If government aid is provided as a *quid pro quo* in exchange for BSC pursuing policies that increase its costs, perhaps the aid packages cited above should not be viewed in isolation without considering these additional obligations. On the other hand, it is precisely the obligation to maintain production and employment in current high-cost locations that keeps total U.K. supply larger than it otherwise would be.

Steel has been a priority industry in France, too. Initial postwar measures were aimed at encouraging mergers to create viable-sized producers. The provision of government loans on favorable terms has been an important policy tool, particularly under the Plan Professional that ran from 1966 to 1971.[29] The loans were made available through the Fonds de Development Economique et Social (FDES), a government institution whose operations initially focused on infrastructure development. The 1966 plan channeled more money to the industry, at favorable interest rates of 3 percent for the first five years and 4 percent for the remainder of the loan maturity. FDES loans represented approximately 46 percent of total investment in the French steel industry over the period 1966 to 1970. Also in the 1960s, another benefit to steel producers was the government practice of rediscounting steel exporters' bills at a rate at least 1.5 percent below the normal discount rate. Complaints by European partners caused this practice to be dropped.

A more comprehensive aid plan was developed when the French steel industry was hit by the recessionary conditions of 1977. In fact, the growth in employment over the period from 1970 to 1977 reported in Table 5 may reflect the effect of policies that merely postponed the inevitable. The government's 1978 rescue plan entailed converting the industry's $9 billion of debts into equity and claiming a majority share of its capital for the state.[30] The government acquired 15 percent directly and the state-run banks another 60 percent. The government also guaranteed payments to private bondholders, a program requiring $1.8 billion in expenditures. This government take-over, billed as a temporary measure until the companies could re-acquire their own shares, involved two large producers, Sacilor and Usinor, who each reported previous year losses of $450 million, and a smaller producer, Chiers Chatillion, which had lost $150 million the preceeding year. The aim of the program is to reduce capacity from 33 million tons to roughly 25.5 million tons by 1983 and to cut the workforce by 20 percent from its 1977 level.

The government also announced a $2 billion industrial adaptation plan, which included steel as well as mining and shipbuilding. Ignoring that program and calculating the interest that otherwise would have been due on debts assumed by the state represents a subsidy element nearly equal to 10 percent of the value of industry output. Such aid has prevented industry output from contracting as rapidly as it otherwise would have been forced to.

Italy represents another case where government intervention has played an important role in the steel industry,[31] and the figures in Table 5 represent a substantial expansion of output in recent years, despite rising energy prices. The major producer, Finsider, is 50 percent owned by the government holding company Instituto per la Ricostruzione Industriale (IRI), and in 1975 accounted for 60 percent of industry output. Within the Finsider group, the most important firm is Italsider, which reported losses of $411 million in 1978. Previously, a second government group, Ente di Gestione per la Aziende (EGAM), existed, with the particular responsibility to promote specialty steel production. In April 1977 it was dissolved, and the steel-making operations were transferred to IRI. Because those companies had lost $43 million in 1975 and were carrying substantial debt loads, too, this acquisition was a mixed blessing to IRI, encouraged by the government through a loan of $100 million.

As in the Japanese case, Finsider has been able to expand output through borrowing, a strategy that yields very high debt-equity ratios. The extent of this borrowing suggests that the government priority assigned to the industry enabled it to raise capital more easily than from private sources due to the implicit government commitment to the industry. A major expansion of capacity occurred with the opening of the Taranto complex in southern Italy. The subsidies available to promote development of the south appear insufficient to attract much private investment in the region, and consequently this form of government aid would appear to be mostly compensatory in nature. Unfortunately, more precise data are not available from which more direct comparisons could be drawn with the British and French cases.

In Germany, limited government participation in the steel industry does exist; Saltzgitter, with 1978 losses of $48 million, and Saarbergwerke are government controlled. However, that factor has not been a dominant force in the industry. Estimates reported in the FTC study indicate that over the period 1960 to 1970, subsidies accounted for 5.2 percent of capital outlays and loan guarantees were available for another 7.3 percent.[32] The subsidy element from this aid represents roughly one percent of the value of sales. Counterbalancing this form of aid has been the German goal of assisting the domestic coal mining industry, particularly by limiting the ability of steel producers to import lower-priced coking coal. The FTC calculates that this disadvantage offsets the other direct financial aids provided to the industry. Germany's shift from being a net exporter to a net importer in 1977 reflects a trend the government apparently has not attempted to alter substantially.

The Canadian steel industry, largely owned by the private sector, also has grown fairly rapidly, as indicated in Table 5. An important aspect of government policy has been the rapid write off of equipment allowed in the manufacturing sector. This provision is particularly beneficial to an industry such as steel that makes large capital outlays, and it undoubtedly has played a role in encouraging the construction of new integrated mills in Canada. Canadian producers report the highest returns on equity of any major OECD country.[33] The small size of the Canadian industry relative to the world market suggests that the international competitive effects of Canadian policies currently are small, though.

U.S. steel production and employment fell over the period 1970 to 1977, and the 1970 base already was below the peak of 1969. The situation has not been reversed since then, as indicated by the certification of roughly 100,000 workers to receive trade adjustment assistance from April 1975 through May 1979.[34] While the payments made to workers under TAA may not appear to help the industry directly, they may well reduce the need to make private provisions for supplementary income during layoffs. More intuitively, if the TAA program were abolished, the steel industry probably would be under greater pressure to increase the supplementary unemployment benefits it provides.

The continued expansion of worldwide capacity coupled with the slack demand conditions in Europe and Japan during 1976 and 1977 led to considerable competition in the U.S. market. As an indication of that competition, in October 1977, the U.S Treasury ruled that Japanese carbon steel plate was being dumped in the United States at a loss of $50 per ton. Obviously that decision represented only a small part of a more general situation. The political pressure generated by increasing import penetration led to the establishment in 1978 of the trigger price system. Imports below the trigger levels, which were set on the basis of average total cost of the most efficient producer, were presumed to indicate dumping, and an accelerated investigation would be initiated in those cases.

Besides the trigger price system, another part of the package designed to help U.S. steel makers was a reduction in the depreciable tax life of steel plants, from 18 to 14 ½ years.[35] The measure was projected to be worth $60 million to U.S. steel producers. By way of comparison, in 1975, comparable tax lives for Italian capital investments were 8 years for blast furnaces and 10 years for plate, sheet and wire rod mills. In France, a 10-year life was assumed, and the declining balance rate that could be claimed was 25 percent. Only Japan and Germany had more comparable 13- to 14-year service lives.[36] These figures indicate that there are significant differences across countries in the ability to generate funds internally.

Of course, the availability of funds is just one part of the relevant comparison: only if labor and all other inputs were identically priced internationally would this be the most significant factor to consider. A 1977 study by the Council on Wage and Price Stability indicates that higher construction costs in the United States work against an expansion of American capacity.[37] The Council also judged that a major reason for declining U.S. competitiveness was a much higher increase in labor costs per unit of output than that experienced in other countries.

Given that the decline in U.S. output can be attributed to several causes, what role has the subsidization of foreign steel played? One way of answering this question is to project the ability of foreign producers to charge lower prices as a result of government subsidization and to calculate how that initial price change alters U.S. prices and output. The model applied here is explained more fully in Appendix B, but the approach used can be summarized fairly concisely. Steel production in the United Kingdom, for example, is not regarded as a perfect substitute for steel produced in the United States due to differences in product quality and reliability of delivery, among other factors. A reduction in the price of U.K. steel will cause some increase in U.S. imports, and a cutback in U.S. purchases of home-produced steel. Further, U.K. imports will fall and foreign exporters will reduce their prices in other markets to sell what was displaced from the British market. U.S. imports from those sources can be expected to rise, and U.S. output and prices will fall on that score, too.

Applying this model to allow for the combined effects of the fairly substantial British and French government aid programs yields an estimated increase in U.S imports of 3 percent and a decline in U.S. output of about 1 percent. Basically, these numbers are not larger because the greatest subsidies are being paid in those countries that account for relatively small shares of the total U.S. import market. The estimates would be somewhat larger if an accepted measure of the role of aid in previous decades were included, particularly in the case of Japan.

THE AUTOMOTIVE INDUSTRY: PASSENGER CARS

Trade and production patterns in the automotive industry have been influenced by a somewhat different set of factors than those identified in the textile and steel industries. Growth trends have been relatively more favorable, too, as reflected in Table 6. Comparisons across industries are somewhat difficult to make because of differences in cyclical factors, though. For instance, 1974 was a boom year for world steel production, but a generally depressed year for auto sales due to the impact of the OPEC oil embargo and gasoline price shock. The unfavorable conditions of 1974 led to additional government assistance to the industry in several European countries.

An important aspect of government intervention has been trade policy. Due to protectionism in foreign markets, U.S firms generally have found it most efficient to establish production facilities abroad and have captured major shares of some of the European markets.

Tax and subsidy measures have played a role in the automotive industry, too. European nations particularly have offered competing investment incentives to attract new plants and employment to their countries. The following comments indicate the scope of these policies and other forms of government intervention in the recent past.

The Japanese growth in production and exports has been the greatest of any of the countries studied, and this growth in exports has been particularly dramatic in the decade of the 1970s. Successful development of the automotive industry has been a priority of the Japanese government, although no government ownership stake exists. Direct loans did not account for a very large share of capital formation, and again fiscal intervention tended to be more important, with provisions for large first-year depreci-

TABLE 6: COMPARATIVE PASSENGER CAR STATISTICS, 1977 (SITC 7321)

	Output (1969 = 100)	Imports (1970 = 100)*	Imports as Share of Consumption*	Exports (1970 = 100)*	Exports as Share of Shipments*	Population per Registered Car
Canada	1.13	2.4 1.2	0.75 0.18	1.3 2.2	0.79 0.06	2.3
France	1.64	2.0 20.3	0.28 0.09	1.5 1.4	0.59 0.18	3.1
Germany	1.10	1.5 7.6	0.33 0.19	1.1 1.1	0.48 0.31	3.0
Italy	0.97	1.2 20.5	0.38 0.04	1.0	0.45 0.18	3.4
Japan	2.08	2.2	0.02	4.1	0.55	5.7
United Kingdom	0.77	4.4	0.45 0.12	0.7	0.36 0.25	3.9
United States	1.11	1.4 1.5	0.25 0.17	2.5 2.7	0.08 0.02	2.0

*Second entry denotes export or import trade exclusive of partners in trading bloc, i.e., for European countries, net out EC trade; for United States and Canada, net out trade with each other.
Sources: Motor Vehicle Manufacturers Association, *Facts and Figures*, and OECD, *Trade by Commodities*, various issues.

ation claims. Government trading policy has been especially important, since the Japanese market was completely closed to foreign competitors until the mid 1960s.[38] Even then, a 35 percent tariff was levied on imports, and limitations on the importation of engines still existed. Controls on direct foreign investment in the industry were not relaxed until 1971, perhaps out of fear that Ford and General Motors would attain the same degree of domination that they exercised in the Japanese market in the 1920s. Liberalizations of controls were limited to new investments and did not include approval for the purpose of buying out existing operations. Consequently, the home market, which was quite small in the initial postwar period, provided a captive testing ground for domestic producers to use in developing products that could meet foreign competition. That market has since grown dramatically, as personal income has increased. While the figures in Table 6 show that Japan still has the lowest auto density of any country studied, further rapid growth is unlikely. MITI has projected that the automotive industry will grow at a slightly slower rate than the economy as a whole over the period through 1985, 5.9 percent, and that despite rapid productivity growth, employment will increase at the annual rate of 0.9 percent.[39]

One characteristic of the earlier growth period was the effort of MITI to encourage mergers and consolidation of the industry around two large producers, Toyota and Nissan. That effort was not entirely successful because Japan still has nine separate producers in a market smaller than that of the United States. Yet, a comparison of the set of aftertax income-to-sales ratios of three comparably sized international auto producers, Toyota, Volkswagon and Renault, shows that in 1978 the respective values were 4.2 percent, 2.0 percent and 0.2 percent.[40] Thus, additional sales to achieve scale economies do not appear to have been generated through a policy of price discounting irrespective of profits earned.

Special tax or subsidy treatment by the government does not appear to be a major determinant of Japan's current competitive position. As special benefits to exporters were dropped in the 1970s, and the appreciation of the yen occurred, Japanese export growth still has been phenomenal, due to increased productivity and the shift in U.S. demand toward smaller, fuel-efficient cars.

European markets also benefited from a policy of protection in the postwar period. The post-Kennedy Round tariff still was 11 percent, a figure reduced gradually from postwar levels of 30 to 40 percent.[41] Stringent trade barriers still exist at a national level: Italy limits imports of Japanese cars to 2,200; France has warned the Japanese against excessive market penetration; and in 1977, the United Kingdom asked Japan to voluntarily limit exports to 11 percent of the market.[42] The initial protection undoubtedly contributed to the decision of U.S. producers to locate production facilities in Europe. Where these operations should be located within Europe has been a decision quite susceptible to government investment incentives. In addition to such generally available aid, government ownership has been an important factor.

The least amount of intervention has occurred in Germany. However, the sharp decline in Volkswagon sales that occurred in 1974 threatened severe regional unemployment problems and called for government action. Since federal and state ownership of VW amounts to 41 percent, the failure to pay a dividend in 1973 and 1974 might have been an easier policy to pursue than under completely private ownership. No special loans were provided to finance the development of new models to replace the Beetle, though. Instead, the federal government committed $87 million to be spent over three years in encouraging new business activities in these areas to provide alternative jobs for those laid off by VW.[43] Thus, little direct assistance was provided to the automotive industry. VW's success in marketing new higher-priced models indicates little likelihood of further government intervention to aid the auto industry in particular.

Examples of where government programs probably have affected the basic decision of how many vehicles to produce instead of merely altering the location of production within Europe can be cited in other European countries. Government-controlled Alfa Romeo joined in the national objective of developing southern Italy and in 1972 constructed a major new assembly plant in Naples. From 1973 to 1978, Alfa Romeo reported positive profits in only a single year.[44] Its 1978 losses were $150 million, which led to a further infusion of government capital of $144 million. Labor problems have kept output well below planned levels. While these problems may be resolved in the future, the more competitive pricing made possible through government equity participation and implicit backing of private loans does have an effect on total world output and international competitive conditions. However, as shown in Appendix B, the smaller the share of the market accounted for by the subsidized producer, the less other producers will be affected by a given price advantage due to government assistance. Consequently, of much greater importance will be the possible extension of aid to the private producer Fiat, which produced six times as many cars as Alfa Romeo in 1977. Proposals debated in July 1980 called for a major government role to fund a portion of Fiat's planned expenditures of $5 billion for research and development and to provide benefits to workers laid off in the downturn of 1980.[45] Fiat lost $120 million in 1979, but a more general deterioration of the Italian situation is reflected in the falling output figures over the 1969–77 period shown in Table 6.

France produces more than twice as many cars as Italy, and therefore French policies are likely to have a larger world impact. Remarkable growth in output is reflected in Table 6. Renault, the nationalized producer, reported low profits throughout the '70s, and subsidies and infusions of capital into the firm have been made regularly. For instance, from 1973 to 1978, $400 million were paid to Renault in subsidies. A more dominant source of subsidy in this situation again would be the ability to earn less than normal rates of return on equity capital.

A more recent goal of the French government appears to be the encouragement of larger producers in the industry, not just Renault but also Peugeot. In 1974, the French government made a loan of $230 million to Citroen for a 15-year period at a 9.75 percent interest rate to make its merger with Peugeot more attractive, a step considered necessary due to Citroen's 1974 losses of $180 million.[47] That merger was carried out in 1976, and in only three years the Citroen operations had become profitable. The French government also encouraged the 1978 purchase by Peugeot-Citroen of Chrysler's European operations in the United Kingdom, France and Spain. Union workers in Britain challenged the merger on grounds that it would reduce the amount of competition in the European automotive market, but the European court dismissed the case. The sale was made for $420 million in cash and stock. Subsidies to Renault already have been cited. In 1979, it acquired a 20 percent interest in Mack Truck and provided $150 million in financing to American Motors, a first step in a series of moves leading to a 46 percent interest in AMC by 1981. That these sums of money would be unlikely to come by in private capital markets seems a warranted judgment given Renault's earnings of $4.0 million in 1977 and $2.2 million in 1978. Part of this action is motivated by the belief that economies of scale in production can be achieved, for example, through sharing common engines and transmissions in the Talbot (Chrysler), Citroen and Peugeot operations. Also, economies of scale in marketing this wider range of products may exist. That the strategy will be successful is a bet that the French government and state-owned banks appear willing to take.

The British situation also is characterized by major government intervention spurred by the 1974 downturn. Due to the impending bankruptcy of British Leyland, the government acquired a majority position in the firm in 1975.[48] An initial infusion of $405 million was made, long-term loans of $1 billion were provided, and guarantees of $405 million were offered, to become available over the period through 1978. Before that period was complete, BL was granted a $2 billion aid package, designed to be the final assistance necessary. But even under the Conservative government elected in 1979, a further $2.39 billion aid package has been approved.[49] Perhaps the magnitude of these requests can be appreciated best by noting that BL's sales in 1978 were $5.9 billion.

Not only did BL face severe problems in the 1974 downturn, but so did Chrysler. An aid package of loans, grants and guarantees was arranged amounting to roughly $380 million, $170 million of which was a grant, $120 million a low interest loan, and $80 million a guarantee to aid Chrysler in restructuring its short-term debt.

The exact size of these aid commitments is difficult to determine because one agreement often has eclipsed another. The Commission of the European Communities has raised no objections, primarily due to the regional employment consequences experienced if major closures were allowed. Undoubtedly, the scale of aid has had an effect on international competitiveness, too. If BL had reported the same return on stockholder equity as Ford Motor of Britain in 1978 for the same volume of sales, prices would have been 6 to 7 percent higher. Such effects would seem particularly important in the European market where transport costs do not form another trade barrier that dwarfs producer price differentials.

The U.S. automotive market was the most open of any producing country during the 1970s. The industry has not received substantial direct aid from the federal government, although the assistance plan for Chrysler implemented in 1980 involved $1.5 billion of federal loan guarantees, under the provision that Chrysler arrange $2 billion in additional financing and concessions. Successive waves of oil price increases in real terms have led to cutbacks in large car production in the United States, and more than 399,000 auto workers laid off have been able to claim trade adjustment assistance benefits through October 1980.[50] Until the recent negotiations by Chrysler to receive local tax relief to justify maintaining current plants in operation, most local incentives had been directed at attracting new entrants into an area, as exemplified by the 1976 bidding to attract Volkswagon's first assembly plant in the United States. (Pennsylvania's aid package was equal to roughly 20 percent of capital value of the investment.[51]) That competition takes on international dimensions as well, including Canadian locations. The comparability of Canadian locations arises from the 1965 Canadian-American Automotive Agreement under which auto manufacturers essentially were able to establish a free trade area. Due to low transportation costs and no tariff barriers, investment incentives to locate on either side of the border can be as important as in Europe. As one recent example, in 1978, Ford announced that it would locate an engine plant in Windsor, Ontario, with an assistance package of $8 million, or 12 percent of the initial investment. Again, general tax provisions that favor manufacturing in Canada, such as rapid write-offs of new equipment, are relevant elements of any overall investment comparison.

What is the net impact of U.S. competitiveness of the various tax and subsidy provisions described above? Recent examples of European investment grants, such as concessions by the United Kingdom and West Berlin to Ford and by Austria to General Motors, probably have had their greatest effect on the location of production within Europe rather than on the overall level of production. To the extent that such aid packages more than offset the disadvantages of inconvenient locations, they increase the profitability of production, and in competitive markets would be expected to generate greater overall productive capacity. To sell the greater output, prices would not rise as fast as otherwise, and sales of nonsubsidized producers would be smaller than otherwise.

Whether this competitive adjustment actually would occur is difficult to predict, although most of the aid programs mentioned have been tied to commitments to maintain existing capacity or to build new plants. However, even if their impact were fully reflected in greater capacity, the competitive effect on production in the United States would not be that great. This conclusion follows for two basic reasons. First, the additional capacity available and utilized as a result of the aid granted generally is not that large relative to existing capacity. Even in the more flagrant cases of Renault and BL, current subsidies plus the implicit aid from foregone returns on government equity amount to roughly 7 and 9 percent of assets, respectively, or 5 and 7 percent of sales. Such a subsidy element is smaller than that identified in the steel industry. Second, these auto producers that have received relatively larger subsidies account for a relatively small share of total market output, less than 10 percent under most favorable conditions. The small market shares accounted for by Renault, and especially by BL, mean that any price advantage they offer will not have a large impact in percentage terms on other producers, even though it may allow the output of these two producers to increase substantially more than otherwise. Even if other European and Japanese producers are assumed to react by cutting prices enough to continue operating at full capacity, the effect on U.S. production still would be a projected decline of less than 1 percent. And this estimate may overstate the severity of the adjustment faced in the United States to the extent that European subsidies allow U.S. domestic producers to buy components more cheaply and thereby to compete more effectively with Japanese producers.

Again, international trade policies appear to play a larger role than tax and subsidy programs. Without a separate study of the issue, the tariff equivalent effect of European limitations on Japanese sales would appear to yield a relative price effect much greater than the 5 to 7 percent range just cited. For instance, limiting Japanese sales to 2,200 cars in the Italian market, where total imports account for 370,000 cars, represents a considerable nontariff barrier to trade. Given these limitations on Japanese sales, the openness of the U.S. market continues to be particularly important in allowing Japanese producers to achieve the economies of scale necessary to be competitive in world markets. Therefore, changes in trade policies, particularly the U.S.-Japanese agreement in 1981 to limit sales in the U.S. market, are likely to dominate the tax and subsidy policies summarized above.

THE PHARMACEUTICAL INDUSTRY

Production and trade patterns in the pharmaceutical industry differ in several respects from those observed in the other industries studied. World output has risen steadily. As shown in Table 7, only Japan and Canada are net importers. Direct subsidies to producing companies generally have not been paid, and government ownership motivated on the grounds of bailing out a failing enterprise is not common either.

TABLE 7: COMPARATIVE PHARMACEUTICAL INDUSTRY STATISTICS (SITC 541)

	Value of Production, 1977 (U.S.$ Millions)	Value of Exports			Value of Imports		
		1977	Percentage of Shipments	1970 = 1.00	1977	Percentage of Apparent Consumption	1970 = 1.00
Canada	707	72	0.10	2.11	228	0.26	2.17
France	3,715	743	0.20	3.23	415	0.12	2.88
Germany	5,296	1,351	0.26	2.76	722	0.15	4.15
Italy	2,493	471	0.19	3.06	378	0.16	2.64
Japan	8,600	180	0.02	2.72	612	0.07	2.83
United Kingdom	2,825	969	0.34	2.89	303	0.14	3.74
United States	14,436	1,116	0.08	2.66	320	0.02	3.67

Sources: OECD, *The Chemical Industry*, various issues, and OECD, *Trade by Commodities*, various issues.

Rather, talk of nationalization has centered on the need to limit private returns in the industry. A fall in pharmaceutical profit margins was reported in most countries during the mid 1970s, but predicting the effect on the industry is no straightforward exercise.

One complicating factor is the industry's high technological base, combined with relatively low energy and material input requirements per dollar of sales. These are some of the reasons why many countries regard it as a priority industry to be encouraged in the 1980s. The higher R&D expenditures in this industry relative to others means that tax treatment of these outlays is a relevant consideration, although to the extent that this research requires relatively more skilled labor than depreciable capital, faster write-offs of capital assets are less important. Also, the riskiness attached to this form of investment suggests that companies will rely on internal financing to a greater extent rather than extensive external borrowing. This generalization holds even in Japan; for the largest pharmaceutical producer, Takeda, the ratio of stockholders equity to total assets is 3½ times greater than the comparable ratio for Nippon Steel.[52] That the length of time for which ethical drugs usually remain profitable is 10 to 12 years underscores the need for continued research expenditures and new product innovation.

With respect to most pharmaceutical products, demand has been characterized as fairly inelastic. Price is not a major consideration in the sale of prescription drugs where the doctor and not the patient decides which drug to prescribe. This situation is changing given the growing importance of generic drugs available from several sources, although in the United States generic prescriptions still accounted for only 12 percent of total prescriptions in 1979.[53] Rather, the major source of competition is through innovation and the development of new products.

The high cost of research and product development means that the ability to spread these costs over foreign sales as well as the domestic market will be important. As in the case of automobiles, nontariff barriers to trade exist. For example, various countries require that any clinical data in support of a new drug application come from studies made within the country, or that a local panel of experts testify to the drug's efficacy, or that production facilities be certified by national inspectors, or that the drug be packaged and labeled in a certain form. Many of these regulations make the location of production facilities abroad often more important than exports and imports. In 1978, roughly 42 percent of the sales of U.S. firms were made abroad, yet exports represented only 8 percent of total U.S. production.[54]

Through the 1960s, restrictions on the introduction of new drugs became more stringent in more countries. A recent review of the pharmaceutical industry suggests that legislation in Canada, Sweden and the United Kingdom is equally as stringent as in the United States.[55] However, the U.S. process to demonstrate that these standards have been met takes significantly more time to complete than in other countries. Because such delays have denied patients treatment with drugs whose safety is accepted elsewhere, the U.S. situation would be justified only if there were substantial gains from keeping unsafe drugs off the market. In one of the few studies to address this issue, Wardell and Lasagna conclude that U.S. policy results in considerable loss to the United States.[56]

Another implication of longer approval times is that firms will require larger staffs and will tie up R&D funds for a longer period of time in order to ensure compliance. These additional fixed costs represent another factor that encourages optimal company size to increase and that argues in favor of a multinational marketing strategy. A second competitive effect is that less production is likely to take place in the United States than otherwise, since U.S. regulations prohibit the export of drugs not approved for use in the United States. Thus, longer approval times not only reduce the return to research expenditures by limiting sales in the United States but also the incentive to produce in the United States.

Tax treatment of earnings from export income and subsidiary operations abroad also is more important in this industry than in the others considered. The reason this factor is so important in pharmaceuticals requires an understanding of the issue of transfer pricing. Material inputs account for a relatively small percentage of total produce value, perhaps only 20 percent.[57] Other costs such as research and development and product promotion represent expenditures companies generally have considerable latitude in allocating to home or foreign operation. In particular, no open market price exists for many patented pharmaceutical products, and therefore there is no easily observable yardstick to determine whether a company is trying to reduce the impact of high tariffs or is attempting to move profits out of high tax jurisdictions and into low tax countries. For instance, a firm may have an incentive to charge a low intracompany transfer price when selling from a high tax country to a low tax country and, conversely, it may levy a much higher price when moving goods from a low tax jurisdiction to a high tax country. Because most tax authorities merely specify that arms-length prices should prevail, i.e., the same price should be charged in an intracompany transaction as would apply to an unrelated party, any price that covers marginal production costs generally provides an acceptable lower bound. In the extreme, this strategy would have the effect of charging all development costs against income in the high tax country and allowing the income from the product developed to be reported in a low tax area. In the case of the United States, a higher tax at home is avoided as long as the foreign income is not repatriated. Such a tax break allows the firm to generate internal funds more easily, which makes the financing of R&D expenditures easier. Schwarzman discusses the low expected payoff to greater R&D expenditures, but he presents regression results that suggest that greater R&D expenditures do result in more new drug approvals and thereby enhance a firm's competitive position.[58]

The United States is the largest producer of pharmaceuticals and also the largest consumer market. The size of this market has meant that the United States is one of the few countries that has developed a full range of pharmaceuticals for domestic consumption and thereby has reduced its dependence on imports to fill certain product areas where no domestic production occurs. U.S. tax laws do provide for the immediate write-off of expenditures incurred in research and development, a slightly more favorable position than exists in most countries. On the other hand, U.S. tax regulations restrict the way expenses can be charged against domestic versus foreign income. These restrictions, plus the vigilance of importing countries, may limit the ability of U.S. producers to use freely the transfer pricing strategies outlined above. While substantial controversy over the application of these provisions still exists, a significant exception to avoid these potential limitations is available through the operation of a possession's corporation.[59] The relevant story to consider deals with the interaction of industrial tax incentives available in Puerto Rico following World War II and the former provisions of Section 931 of the Internal Revenue Code. Under this section, if a corporation derived at least 80 percent of its income from operations in a U.S. possession and if at least 50 percent of its income was derived from an active trade or business, then that income did not incur a U.S. corporate tax liability.[60] If the income were earned from manufacturing operations that also qualified for income tax exemption in the possession, then taxation of the income could be avoided entirely. When dividends were paid to the parent, a U.S. tax liability was incurred, and therefore the possession's corporation generally accumulated its earnings to be brought back tax free when it was liquidated into its parent.

The Tax Reform Act of 1976 modified these provisions and created a slightly different structure for possessions' corporations under Section 936 of the Internal Revenue Code. Dividends from a wholly owned 936 subsidiary no longer added to the U.S. parent's corporate tax liability, but any withholding tax levied on those dividends could not be claimed as a foreign tax credit. On the other hand, income from the investment of possessions' corporation earnings in foreign outlets such as the Eurodollar market no longer avoided U.S. corporate tax. Thus, there was more incentive to repatriate funds to the United States. In 1976, the government of Puerto Rico altered the form of its tollgate tax applied to dividends paid out of Puerto Rican income and made it applicable on dividends paid to U.S. parent corporations. Because the exact terms of the tollgate tax have been subject to considerable bargaining and negotiation, how much these changes have reduced the attraction of operating through a 936 corporation cannot be calculated yet. From 10-K reports filed in 1978 by U.S. parent corporations with the Securities and Exchange Commission, the benefit of the 936 provisions to U.S. pharmaceutical producers appears to have allowed a tax saving, on average, of 10 percent of pretax parent income, or roughly 2 percent of the value of sales.

The competitive advantage to U.S. pharmaceutical producers may not be that great if producers in other countries have similar options available, though. Horst's figures regarding the taxation of export income already have been cited to indicate that tax burdens in foreign countries can be quite low. The tax burden on income from subsidiary operations in low tax countries may be even lower. In order that multinational firms take advantage of such tax incentives, the host country must be sufficiently stable politically and economically. Additional factors encouraging this strategy are transfer pricing rules that allow most development costs to be deducted by the parent corporation in a high tax jurisdiction, and tax laws such that passive or portfolio investment income can be accumulated abroad free of tax by both the home and the host country. In the American case, Puerto Rico has been an attractive location for U.S. producers, while Ireland and the Mezzogiorno of Italy have provided a convenient base for operations within the European market.[61] New businesses are exempt for a 15-year period from income and corporate profit taxes on profits generated from the export of goods manufactured in Ireland. Dividends paid out of these profits are exempt from Irish taxes as well. In the case of the Mezzogiorno, firms receive a 10-year exemption from the local income tax and a 50 percent reduction in the corporate income tax. These two locations, then, provide an attractive option for foreign-based producers.

The following survey gives a somewhat broader indication of the extent to which these conditions are met abroad.[62] For instance, German-owned subsidiaries in less-developed countries, or in countries with which Germany has signed a tax treaty, are exempt from German taxation. However, the parent firm's ability to allocate income to a subsidiary has been more limited since 1972, and Germany also has adopted provisions similar to U.S. treatment of passive income under Subpart F of the Internal Revenue Code.[63] Conversely, under the territorial system of taxation applied by France, 95 percent of foreign-earned income is exempt from French taxation (100 percent if not repatriated). Also, French enforcement of transfer pricing practices is not as stringent as in the United States or Germany. The Italian system also approaches the French territorial system, since the local income tax is assessed only on Italian source income. Japanese foreign subsidiary earnings are taxable when repatriated, but Japan has no provision similar to Subpart F of the U.S. code limiting the ability to accumulate passive income abroad free of tax. If the parent company also has operations in Western economies, because of Japan's relatively lower corporate income tax rates, the parent is likely to have generated excess foreign tax credits it can use to offset any tax due on income repatriated from a tax-haven subsidiary. Japanese regulations also are more generous in allowing expenses to be borne by the parent corporation instead of foreign affiliates. Only in the case of a British subsidiary operating abroad does a higher corporate tax burden seem likely, due to more careful British regulation of transfer pricing practices and to limitations on the ability to accumulate passive income abroad.

These tax advantages represent the major benefit available to pharmaceutical producers. Other government measures with respect to required proof of safety and efficacy before a drug is introduced, or price controls imposed on national health system purchases, instead handicap producers to varying degrees. In assessing the competitive impact of these various factors combined, few precise conclusions can be drawn. To the extent that U.S. tax breaks such as the possession's corporation provisions offset greater regulatory delays and encourage production in the United States, U.S. exports might be expected to grow faster than the production of U.S. affiliates abroad. On the other hand, if faster drug approval times in foreign countries offset potentially less favorable tax treatment, for example, the production of foreign affiliates might increase more rapidly than U.S. exports. Because the majority of U.S. affiliate sales are in developed countries where the overall growth of the market is not too different from that in the United States, the following comparison provides some evidence of the relative importance of the various possibilities mentioned above: of total pharmaceutical sales by U.S.-controlled firms in 1970, 6.1 percent were exported from the United States and 25.6 percent were sales by foreign affiliates, net of imported materials from the parent corporation; in 1978, the corresponding figures were 6.3 percent for exports and 35.4 percent for net sales of affiliates. The necessity, or relative attractiveness, of producing abroad appears to have increased markedly over the past decade.

THE COMPUTER INDUSTRY

The computer industry is the fastest growing and most rapidly changing of any of the industries studied. In fact, the pace of its growth and the diversity of new products and processes developed may explain why comparable trade and production statistics are difficult to obtain and to interpret over time. The present picture of world production and trade is not too difficult to summarize in general qualitative terms, though, as indicated in Table 8. U.S. producers, led by IBM, have a commanding market position not just in the United States but throughout the world. This position is maintained through exports from the United States and production abroad; 53 percent of IBM's total revenue in 1979 was accounted for by operations abroad.

The multinational orientation of the computer industry is similar to that reported in the pharmaceutical industry, motivated from the incentive to spread large product development costs over a high volume of output. For instance, in 1979 IBM's expenditures on R&D were $1.4 billion, or nearly 6 percent of revenue.[64] The limited home markets of many foreign countries, even when protected by trade barriers and government procurement policies to improve the profitability of home producers,

TABLE 8: COMPARATIVE COMPUTER INDUSTRY STATISTICS
(SIC 3573)

	Year	Production	Exports	Imports	Exports Share of Shipments	Imports Share of Apparent Consumption	Share of Installed Capacity, U.S. Owned Producers
		(Millions of Dollars)					
France	1975	870	354	495	0.41	0.49	0.74
	1976	1,021	412	569	0.40	0.48	(1975)
Germany	1975	1,068	492	571	0.46	0.50	0.69
	1978	2,325	1,000	995	0.43	0.43	(1977)
Italy	1975	243	152	344	0.63	0.79	0.79
	1978	402	254	459	0.63	0.76	(1977)
Japan	1975	1,781	133	325	0.07	0.16	0.43
	1978	2,997	209	547	0.07	0.16	(1979)
United Kingdom	1975	578	403	641	0.70	0.79	0.58
	1978	801	560	946	0.70	0.80	(1976)
United States	1975	8,433	2,229	129	0.26	0.02	
	1979	20,850	5,250	960	0.25	0.06	

Sources: Country Market Surveys, computers and peripheral equipment, and U.S. Department of Commerce, *1980 U.S. Industrial Outlook*.

have put foreign producers in a difficult competitive position. One common response abroad has been to subsidize domestic development costs. The scale of these assistance programs is recounted in the summary below. While predicting the competitive effect from these development subsidies again is quite imprecise, past analyses suggest a more systematic relationship between R&D expenditures and innovation than appears to be the case in the pharmaceutical industry. For instance, in a 1971 study, Harman estimated that a 1 percent increase in R&D expenditures led to a 3.5 percent improvement in computer performances, as measured in terms of computational time and memory capacity.[65] Subsidies that allow higher R&D expenditures therefore improve a firm's competitive position in the international market. However, the very large outlays necessary to support a domestic computer industry producing a full range of products suggests a logical reason why countries such as Canada and Italy have found it difficult to develop an indigenous producer.

This review does not consider the related electronics industry, although some integrated producers such as IBM and Nippon Electric Company of Japan do produce a portion of their component inputs. In November 1979, the U.S. International Trade Commission released a study of the semiconductor industry that provides an account of international practices in that intermediate industry, and that material will not be repeated here.[66]

Although their 1978 share of the world computer market was only 8 percent, the Japanese are increasingly seen as possible challengers to the U.S. position of market leader. No direct government ownership exists in the Japanese case, but government controls of imports and foreign investment in Japan have combined with government financial support to promote domestic production. MITI views the computer industry as a vital national interest that should receive as much government protection as the defense industry in the United States.[67] The combination of output of U.S. subsidiaries in Japan and exports from the United States together accounted for 43 percent of the Japanese market in 1979, a matter of concern to the government.[68]

To obtain advanced technology in the 1960s the government encouraged patent licensing and technology transfer agreements with American producers, but attempted to rule out direct foreign control of operations in Japan.[69] Because of its strong position in holding basic patents, IBM was able to convert its yen investment to dollar-based investment in its wholly owned subsidiary in Japan in 1960, which enabled IBM to remit dividends in foreign exchange under the basic laws covering foreign investment and foreign exchange. That authorization was granted in exchange for IBM's willingness to license its patents to 13 Japanese producers. In May 1976, investment controls governing the computer industry were liberalized, and American firms previously forced to license technology appear likely to enter into direct production and sales.

One important element of Japanese policy has been the establishment of the Japan Electronic Computer Company (JECC), financed largely by the Japan Development Bank. JECC does not produce computers, but rather acts as an intermediary to buy computers from Japanese manufacturers and then lease them to customers. The facility is particularly important because producer financing of leasing agreements can be expensive to obtain, since leases containing 30- or 90-day cancellation clauses represent a relatively risky loan for banks. One disadvantage of the leasing scheme became apparent as new models were introduced and old ones returned to JECC. Manufacturers had the obligation to buy these machines back from JECC. In the late 1960s, a measure was adopted to allow 15 percent of the value of sales to JECC to be put into a tax free reserve to cover losses that might arise when models were bought back from

JECC. That figure was later raised to 20 percent, and in 1978 companies were allowed to set aside even larger reserves if they could demonstrate larger buy-back obligations.

General measures to promote research and development in the industry are a 25 percent deduction for expenditures in excess of a base year amount and additional first-year depreciation allowances up to one-third of the value of the investment in plant and equipment. Subsidies of up to 30 percent are available to companies marketing new series of computers or developing prototypes. Over the period 1972-77, MITI provided development subsidies of roughly $400 million to improve Japanese hardware capabilities.[70] This amount represented 2.5 percent of sales by the major domestic producers. In comparison, private R&D expenditures of American firms averaged 5 to 8 percent of receipts. Therefore, the government appears to have been an important partner in allowing the Japanese to close the hardware gap with U.S. producers, but the Japanese share of their home market has increased by only 3 percentage points, from 54 to 57. Also, as shown in the discussion of other country markets, this rate of subsidization is less than that available in most European countries.

The growing importance of software elements in any system implies that a substantial improvement in the Japanese competitive position also will require improved software design and support. In 1978, the Japanese announced a program to encourage software development, with projected government subsidies of $100 million through 1983. Private development expenditures were projected to be five times that amount. Because a major share of Japanese software research has been in developing the ability to process nonalphabetic kanji characters, the competitive implications in current major markets outside Japan are not that great. Also, these developments are being matched by American competitors in the Japanese market.

Finally, a policy common to most governments has been a preference for domestically owned producers in making public procurements. While the United States follows this practice as well, it would not appear to be much of a market distortion in the U.S. case because the private sector also buys almost exclusively American systems. In foreign countries, the difference between public and private practices is considerable. In Japan, domestic manufacturers account fo 94 percent of public-sector purchases, in contrast to 50 percent in the private sector.[71] If the marginal cost of making such sales were judged to be 50 percent of the revenue received, the benefit or subsidy element to Japanese producers would have been about $90 million in 1977, or roughly 3.5 percent of sales. Thus, public procurement easily can be more important than direct subsidy.

The British government's major intervention in the computer industry has been centered in the production of International Computers Limited (ICL). This corporation was formed in 1968 by a merger between International Computers and Tabulators Limited and the English Electric Company, Limited, which the government encouraged through acquiring a 10 percent equity stake. This ownership share was expanded to 24.5 percent, but the National Enterprise Board sold the government's interest in 1979.

The government consistently has made R&D grants to ICL. For instance, the OECD reports that over the period 1971 to 1974, £40 million ($100 million) were made available.[72] Again, government procurement practices have been important, particularly the use of single tender contracts that effectively guarantee that all large computers purchased by the central government are produced by ICL. Since central government purchases represent 15 percent of the U.K. market, the policy amounts to an important subsidy to ICL, roughly 9 percent of total receipts in 1972.[73] Combined with the other direct grants, government aid may account for nearly 15 percent of the value of output.

Despite this intervention, ICL's share of installed capacity in the European market has fallen from 10.7 percent in 1973 to 9.2 percent in 1978.[74]

The French commitment to promote domestic computer production is signified by its assistance to the Companie Internationale Informatique (CII), formed in 1966. This government action would appear to be in response to General Electric's 1964 purchase of Machines Bull, a move that eliminated any major French-owned producer from the world market. The Sixth Plan covering the years 1971 to 1975 generally provided for government grants of 50 percent of private research and development, and it aided CII in particular by granting it an interest free loan of FF 150 million ($30 million), five-year credits from the FDES at a rate of FF 40 million per year, and preferential access to public contracts.[75] This intervention did not guarantee a commercially successful company, and in 1976 CII merged with Honeywell-Bull, the company that followed General Electric's exit from the computer industry.[76] The French claimed 53 percent ownership of the new company and established an aid plan that provided $250 million in direct subsidies and guaranteed $800 million of government purchases over the period 1976–79. The plan reflected a significant government commitment to domestic production of a full range of computers. Currently, attempts are under way to renegotiate the agreement joining Honeywell and CII, but the prospects for an independent CII do not appear bright. CII-Bull sales in 1978 were almost $1.0 billion, while IBM France's sales were $2.5 billion.

German involvement in the computer industry over the past 15 years includes a 1967 program to encourage computer usage in general and to promote development of Siemens' large computers. Efforts to create a home market through promotional activities are important because most countries lag behind the United States in terms of the ratio of computer usage to GDP or workforce. Subsequent plans have included substantial aid to the industry. For instance, R&D grants to the data processing industry over the period 1971 to 1975 averaged $90 million per year and included provisions to fund 50 percent of private research and development and 40 percent of software development costs.[77] Such grants have not necessarily yielded large payoffs, though. AEG Telefunken received $40 million without achieving its goal of developing a large mainframe computer. The 1976–79 plan again called for federal grants equal to 50 percent of the cost of work by public research establishments. The total budget of the plan was Dm 1,575 million ($700 million), with one-third of the budget to support research and development and a major share to promote data processing generally.[78]

The major German producer, Siemens, has expanded its share of the European market from 2.5 percent of installed capacity in 1973 to 3.9 percent in 1978.[79] Siemens is reported to be buying its largest computers from the Japanese firm Fujitsu (also linked with Amdahl), an indication of the specialization and cooperation that may be necessary if independent national producers are to remain viable.

The European nations periodically have attempted to encourage joint production to ensure sufficient scale of operation and research expenditures to compete effectively with U.S. and Japanese producers. In 1973, UNIDATA was formed by Siemens, Phillips and CII, but the group subsequently collapsed in 1975. During that period, the European Commission attempted to limit the availability of government aids to the cases in which producers agreed to collaborate. More recently, though, almost any aid scheme has been accepted on the grounds that most compettiton is not with other European producers but with foreigners. In November 1979, a joint commitment to adopt common standards among European producers was announced, but the outcome of that effort cannot be evaluated yet.

The development of the computer industry in the United States has also been greatly aided by government involvement.[80] The role differs from that in other countries, though. Development contracts have been oriented around particular projects, rather than the funding of an ongoing research institute, or grants for commercial research and development. Demand for greater computational power on the part of the military has provided an impetus for developing new systems. Aside from this developmental role, government purchases account for over 10 percent of the domestic computer market. These purchases have helped provide a sufficiently large market for products to allow scale economies to be achieved. While not all defense related research and production has a direct commercial application, even a partial spillover is important when total expenditures are large. Estimates by Frost and Williams project that military spending for computer hardware will be $8.5 billion over the period 1980 to 1984 and that military software expenditures will be $50 billion during the same period.[81] Even if that scale of spending does not materialize, this market appears to be quite large.

If U.S. producers do face a competitive disadvantage as a result of more direct foreign subsidy programs, how great an impact have they had to absorb? The figures in Table 8 show that, aside from Germany, the United States has experienced the greatest percentage increase in exports from 1975 to 1978. Imports as a share of apparent consumption have dropped slightly in Italy and more so in Germany, but the U.S. market share remains dominant. Thus, if the major impact has been on retarding the rate of growth of U.S. exports, the effect to date does not appear to be large. This situation may well change in the future as competitors establish better sales and service networks, but this is a process not directly related to most development subsidies currently available.

Notes

1   A summary of the recent history of this agreement is given in U.S. Congress, House Committee on Ways and Means, Subcommittee on Trade, *Background Materials on the Multifiber Agreement,* 95th Cong., 2nd sess., 1978, WMCP, 95-62.

2   The following overview and figures cited through 1974 are drawn from the account given by Caroline Pestieau, *The Canadian Textile Policy: A Sectoral Trade Adjustment Strategy?* (Quebec: C.D. Howe Research Institute, 1976).

3   Donald B. Keesing and Martin Wolf, *Textile Quotas Against Developing Countries* (London: Trade Policy Research Center, 1980), pp. 59, 96.

4   The historical facts cited here are taken from the summary of Caroline Miles, "Protection of the British Textile Industry," in *Public Assistance to Industry, Protection and Subsidies in Britain and Germany,* ed. W.M. Corden and G. Fels (Boulder: Westview Press, 1976), pp. 184-213.

5   Commission of the European Communities, *Fourth Report on Competition Policy* (Brussels, 1975), p. 88.

6   Ministry of International Trade and Industry, *Japan's Industrial Structure—A Long-Range Vision,* 1978 edition (Tokyo, 1978), pp. 33-34.

7   Several of the following measures are reported in *Nihon Keizai,* October 1, 1977, p. 3.

8   Joseph Pechman and Keimei Kaizuka, "Taxation," in *Asia's New Giant,* eds. Hugh Patrick and Henry Rosovsky (Washington, D.C.: Brookings Institution, 1976), pp. 353-354. The authors also report that in 1972 a special deduction that could be taken against export income was cut sharply.

9   Commission of the European Communities, *Second Report on Competition Policy* (Brussels, 1973), pp. 89-91.

10 European Commission, *Fourth Report,* pp. 89-91.

11 Axel Neu, "Protection of the German Textile Industry," in *Public Assistance to Industry,* p. 181.

12 Keesing and Wolf, *Textile Quotas,* pp. 61-69.

13 Recent textile market developments are recounted in "Common Market Sets Antidumping Duties on Some U.S. Yarns," *Wall Street Journal,* September 21, 1980.

14 See U.S. Department of Commerce, Industry and Trade Administration, Office of Textiles, *Cotton, Wool and Man-Made Fiber Bilateral Performance Report* (Washington, D.C., 1979).

15 U.S. Department of Commerce, *Sharpening Government's Response to Plant Closings* (Washington, D.C., 1979).

16 U.S. Federal Trade Commission, *Staff Report on the United States Steel Industry and Its International Rivals* (Washington, D.C., 1977).

17 MITI, *Japan's Industrial Structure,* pp. 33-34.

18 Excellent background material is available in the FTC *Staff Report,* and in Eugene Kaplan, *Japan, the Government-Business Relationship* (Washington, D.C.: U.S. Department of Commerce, 1972).

19 Pechman and Kaizuka, "Taxation," p. 358.

20 U.S. Congress, Office of Technology Assessment, *Technology and Steel Industry Competitiveness* (Washington, D.C., 1980), p. 82.

21 MITI, *Japan's Industrial Structure,* p. 19.

22 U.S. Congress, House Committee on Ways and Means, Subcommittee on Trade, Task Force Report, *United States—Japan Trade,* 95th Cong., 2nd sess., 1979, p. 74, WMPC, 95-110.

23 Putnam, Hayes and Bartlett, Inc., *Economics of International Steel Trade* (Newton, Mass., 1977), p. 37.

24 Commission of the European Communities, *Twelfth General Report on the Activities of the European Community* (Brussels, 1979), p. 147.

25 Ibid., p. 94.

26 This historical material is drawn from the FTC, *Staff Report,* pp. 427-435.

27 The following figures come from British Steel Corporation, *Annual Report and Accounts, 1978-1979.*

28 Cited in Kenneth Walters and Joseph Monsen, "State-owned business abroad: new competitive threat," *Harvard Business Review* (March-April 1979), p. 164.

29 FTC, *Staff Report,* pp. 427-437.

30 "Giscard steels himself for nationalization," *The Economist,* September 23, 1978, p. 95.

31 FTC, *Staff Report,* pp. 416-427.

32 Ibid., p. 414.

33 Office of Technology Assessment, *Technology and Steel,* p. 127.

34 Department of Commerce, *Sharpening Government's Response.*

35 "Big Steel's Liquidation," *Business Week,* September 17, 1979, p. 92.

36 These figures are from George Kopits, *International Comparison of Tax Depreciation Practices* (Paris: OECD, 1975), pp. 42, 73, 102, 113.

37 Executive Office of the President, Council on Wage and Price Stability, *Prices and Costs in the United States Steel Industry* (Washington, D.C., 1977).

38 Trade and investment policies are summarized in Shotaro Kamiya, *My Life With Toyota* (Tokyo: Toyota Motor Sales Company, Ltd., 1976) and in Kaplan, *Japan*.

39 MITI, *Japan's Industrial Structure,* pp. 33-34.

40 "The 500 Largest Industrial Corporations Outside of the U.S.," *Fortune,* August 13, 1979, pp. 194-203.

41 Eric Toder, *Trade Policy and the U.S. Automobile Industry* (New York: Praeger, 1977), p. 19.

42 "Japanese Cars' Success Worries Europe, Too," *Wall Street Journal,* November 17, 1980.

43 Commission of the European Communities, *Fifth Report on Competition Policy* (Brussels, 1976), p. 83-84.

44 Walters and Monsen, "State-owned business," p. 166.

45 "Italy Readies Plan to Help Alfa, Fiat Cope with Competition," *Wall Street Journal,* July 21, 1980.

46 Walters and Monsen, "State-owned business," p. 166.

47 European Commission, *Fifth Report,* pp. 82-84.

48 Ibid., pp. 84-85 for aid to BL and to Chrysler.

49 "U.K. Approves Aid of $2.39 Billion for State-Owned BL," *Wall Street Journal,* January 27, 1981.

50 Trade Adjustment Assistance Office, telephone conversation.

51 For a comparison of this case with Canadian policy, see Robert Niehaus, *The Canada-Ford Deal* (Washington, D.C.: Northeast-Midwest Institute, 1978).

52 "The 500 Largest Industrial Corporations."

53 "Generic Prescriptions in the United States," *Scrip,* May 10, 1980, p. 16.

54 Pharmaceutical Manufacturers' Association, *Annual Survey Report, 1978-1979* (Washington, D.C., 1980).

55 Barrie James, *The Future of the Multinational Pharmaceutical Industry to 1990* (New York: Wiley, 1977), p. 100. Other experts also might cite Australia, Germany and Japan as countries with stringent safety and efficacy standards. The point here is simply that U.S. standards, as contrasted to the process by which they are met, do not represent an unusual barrier to new product development.

56 William Wardell and Louis Lasagna, *Regulation and Drug Development* (Washington, D.C.: American Enterprise Institute, 1975).

57 *Marketing Guide to the Pharmaceutical Industry* (Westport, Conn.: Technomic Publishing, 1970), p. 58.

58 David Schwarzman, *Innovation in the Pharmaceutical Industry* (Baltimore: Johns Hopkins University Press, 1976).

59 This background is given in U.S. Department of the Treasury, *The Operation and Effect of the Possessions' Corporation System of Taxation* (Washington, D.C., 1978).

60 Income from an active trade or business should be contrasted to passive income from investment in other companies or financial assets (for instance, interest, dividends, rents, or royalties).

61 Arthur Andersen & Co., *Pocket Guide to European Corporate Taxes, Third Edition* (1975), pp. 32-35.

62 The following summary comments are drawn from Gary Hufbauer, "The Taxation of Export Profits," *National Tax Journal* (March 1975), pp. 43-60.

63 Essentially, Subpart F limits the ability to earn and to accumulate income abroad in low tax countries by assuming for U.S. tax purposes that a portion of certain types of foreign income are received by the U.S. owner regardless of the actual repatriations made. Types of income included in this limitation are: personal holding company income (dividends, interest, royalties, and other passive income); income derived from sales or purchases from related persons if the property is produced and sold for use outside the country in which the controlled foreign corporation (CFC) is incorporated; and service income from managerial or technical services on behalf of a related person outside the country of CFC incorporation.

64 *IBM Annual Report, 1979.*

65 Alvin Harman, *The International Computer Industry* (Cambridge, Mass.: Harvard University Press, 1971).

66   U.S. International Trade Commission, *Competitive Factors Influencing World Trade in Integrated Circuits,* USITC Publication 1013 (Washington, D.C., 1979).

67   Chalmers Johnson, *Japan's Public Policy Companies* (Washington, D.C.: American Enterprise Institute, 1978), p. 58.

68   "Japanese Market Opens Wider than Ever to Foreign-Made Computers," *Electronic Data Processing Japan Report,* January 31, 1978.

69   An excellent review of these developments is given in Kaplan, *Japan.*

70   "Changing Pattern in Government Support of the Japanese Computer Industry," *EDP Japan Report,* August 21, 1978.

71   This figure for 1977 is reported in "Japanese Market Opens Wider than Ever."

72   OECD, *Selected Industrial Policy Instruments, Objectives and Scope* (Paris, 1978), p. 178.

73   Figures from M.B. Krauss, "Quantification of the Effects of Non-tariff Barriers in the Major Trading Countries," submitted to the U.S. Department of Labor (mimeographed) 1978, are used to make this estimate.

74   "European Strategies to Fight IBM," *Business Week,* December 17, 1979, p. 73.

75   European Commission, *Second Report,* p. 94.

76   Commission of the European Communities, *Sixth Report on Competition Policy* (Brussels, 1977), p. 121.

77   European Commission, *Second Report,* pp. 94–95.

78   European Commission, *Sixth Report,* p. 122.

79   "European Strategies," p. 73.

80   Much of this summary material is drawn from John Soma, *The Computer Industry, An Economic-Legal Analysis of its Technology and Growth* (Lexington, Mass.: D.C. Heath, 1976).

81   Cited in *Computers* (Haymarket Publications), November 22, 1979.

Summary and Conclusions 4

This study has considered the international competitive effects of aggregate tax burdens and subsidies in six major industrial countries and the United States, as well as the effects of taxes and subsidies in five important industries.

At the aggregate level, U.S. tax burdens, as measured in terms of shares of gross domestic product, are moderate compared to the other countries studied. Only in Japan do taxes account for a smaller share of GDP. However, allowing for government expenditures that assist or subsidize production gives a different picture of the net effect of government fiscal intervention on international competitiveness. By subtracting the benefits afforded by various subsidy and expenditure programs, net tax burden figures are derived which suggest that the result of government fiscal intervention is to confront U.S. producers with relatively higher costs of labor and capital. Other things equal, this tends to discourage investment, employment and production in the United States. This view represents a snapshot at a single point in time, and recent tax policy changes in the United States and elsewhere may alter these rankings.

Because not all industries are impacted equally by government tax and subsidy policies, five separate industry studies were made. Of course, these brief studies do not provide an exhaustive treatment of all the relevant factors within each industry, nor do they capture all the repercussions throughout the economy from government intervention. Nevertheless, several summary observations can be drawn with respect to the primary impact of the dominant forms of government aid.

Textile assistance programs exist in practically all of the countries studied. Yet, such aid generally represents a small share of the value of domestic output because assistance traditionally has been made available only to the most severely impacted producers. Trade policies have played a much larger role in determining the rate of contraction of employment likely to occur. Both the United States and the European countries rely on the bilateral agreements negotiated under the Multifiber Agreement to limit the growth rate of imports from developing countries. More recently, the European nations have imposed dumping duties on manmade fibers from the United States, which are not covered by the MFA. The growth rate of U.S. imports had been sharply lower than that of most of the other countries through the past decade. Even through the 1960s, the total value of imports into the United States grew less rapidly than in the other countries studied. However, renegotiation of the MFA may alter these trends.

The steel industry has been characterized by a much larger scale of government fiscal intervention. For instance, the Japanese designated steel as an important industry in the 1950s and '60s and promoted its development through favorable tax policies. Examples of more recent and more direct government intervention are Bristish aid to BSC and the French government's role in restructuring its steel industry. Yet, even this level of involvement amounting to several million dollars of assistance annually appears unlikely to have had a major impact on U.S. producers, primarily because of the small share of the U.S. market accounted for by these foreign producers. From the standpoint of necessary contraction of the European industry, and with respect to the likelihood that foreign sales no longer made in Europe will be deflected to the United States, a more important policy step is the EC's 1978 negotiation of quantitative import controls. If European costs continue to rise more rapidly than in other producing nations, the commitment to maintain 1976 import shares will represent an ever greater benefit to European producers.

Passenger car output has grown at a phenomenal rate in the postwar period, particularly outside the United States as foreign incomes rose and first-time buyers entered the market. Trade patterns have changed rapidly as well. For instance, the United States was a net exporter of passenger cars in 1952, but by 1960 imports were three times as great as exports, accounting for 6 percent of the market. In 1970, imports claimed 18 percent of the U.S. market, while in 1979 the comparable figure was 23 percent. The dominance of Japanese exports, at 70 percent of the total U.S. import market in 1979, has been a phenomenon of the 1970s, well after major government provisions to encourage output or exports had been phased out. With respect to the competitive impact on U.S. production, even the scale of subsidies available to BL and Renault has not explained much of the decline of U.S. output. Again, the future course of trade policies in the United States and Europe will be a more important determinant of relative prices confronting U.S. producers and consumers. Just as in the case of steel, European quantitative controls are likely to provide ever greater protection.

In the pharmaceutical industry, international competitiveness has not been influenced by subsidy policies particularly, but tax measures have affected the ability of firms to generate funds internally. National production and packaging regulations often limit the ability to trade pharmaceutical products in final dosage form, but the declining role of bulk exports from the United States relative to U.S. subsidiary production abroad suggests that the necessity or advantage of foreign production outweighs U.S. tax incentives to produce and export from Puerto Rico. With respect to the ability of U.S. producers to maintain a lead in developing commercially successful innovations, the U.S.-controlled share of the value of world output has fallen since 1970 from roughly 35 percent to 31 percent.

The electronic data processing or computer industry has been characterized by a major amount of support in product development grants and government procurement preferences. Such assistance programs in foreign countries largely have forestalled U.S. producers gaining an even more prominent worldwide position than they already hold. In fact, a slight decline in the U.S.-controlled share of the market has occurred in Japan. The growth of U.S. exports has not been as rapid as the growth in foreign markets, in part due to greater output of U.S. subsidiaries abroad which do not face the same trade barriers that U.S. exports do. If changes favorable to the United States are to occur, one important element will be government commitments to more open procurement policies, since those policies generally have provided more aid than direct subsidies.

These summary comments highlight the primary competitive effects of tax and subsidy policies abroad relative to those in the United States. While foreign governments often provide large amounts of aid, these expenditures have had relatively minor impact on U.S. producers in many cases. The costly nature of such aid, with no guaranteed economic or political payoff, suggests why there has been a growing trend in many industries toward greater direct intervention to control trade and to protect home producers. If this trend continues, the concerns of the 1970s over subsidized foreign production can be expected to shift to issues of market access and the deflection of trade that closed markets may cause. In such an environment, the United States will have to increase its efforts to reduce the effects of discriminatory practices of foreign governments on U.S. producers if U.S. firms are to compete on an equitable and fair basis at home and in export markets.

Appendixes

APPENDIX A.
Summary of Tax and Subsidy Programs, and Historical Trade Data

TABLE A-1. INTERNATIONAL TAX SYSTEMS AND INCENTIVES, 1978

	Basic Corporate Income Tax Rate	General Depreciation Practices and Investment Tax Credits	Incentives for Particular Regions	Incentives for Particular Sectors
Canada	46% federal + 0–5% provincial.	7% investment tax credit. Depreciation, declining balance allowed; straight line rates buildings 5%, machinery 20%.	Investment tax credit 20% in Maritime Provinces, 10% in other development areas. Special provincial income tax deductions in Ontario and Quebec. Employment tax credits for hiring unemployed, $2/hr. in Maritimes.	40% corporate income tax and 50% depreciation of machinery in manufacturing, first year. 2-yr. write-off assets used in pollution control. 10% R&D tax credit plus 150% deduction for incremental R&D expenditure.
France	50%.	depreciation, declining balance allowed; straight line rates buildings 5%, machinery 10–20%.	25% immediate write-off for industrial buildings in less-developed areas. Exemption from local business tax that can range up to 8% of investment.	50% depreciation allowance for buildings used solely in R&D.
Germany	56% undistributed profits, 36% distributed profits + municipal trade taxes 10–18%.	Depreciation immobile buildings, 2% straight line. Declining balance allowed for machinery; straight line rates 20% computers, 10% equipment.	Special depreciation on fixed assets in Berlin and border zone; up to 50% write-off in first 5 years above normal straight line depreciation.	Special depreciation on pollution control and R&D equipment; up to 50% write-off in first 5 years above normal straight line depreciation.
Italy	25% + local income taxes ≈ 14.7%.	Depreciation practices, accelerated depreciation allowed for first 3 years; straight line rates buildings 3–7%, machinery 16–18%.	10-year local income tax exemption and reduction to ½ corporate income tax for new industries and conversions in Mezzogiorno. 10-year local tax exemption for investment in other depressed areas; 70% exemption of any income from local tax if that amount invested in Mezzogiorno. Exemption from employer's social security contributions on new employees in Mezzogiorno through 1986.	

TABLE A-1 CONTINUED

Japan	40% undistributed profits, 30% distributed profits + local enterprise and inhabitants taxes 15–20%.	Depreciation practices, declining balance allowed; straight line rates buildings 1.6–2.5%, equipment 7–25%.	Pollution control equipment qualifies for large additional first-year write-off.
United Kingdom	52%.	Depreciation, industrial buildings 50% initial year, 4% thereafter; machinery 100% or 25% declining balance.	
United States*	48% + state income tax 0–12%.	Depreciation, declining balance allowed; straight line rates buildings 2.5%–4%, equipment 8–20%. Investment tax credit 10% of qualifying investments.	Immediate write-off of R&D capital costs, 60-month write-off of pollution control equipment.

* The U.S situation has been altered by provisions of the Economic Recovery Tax Act of 1981. Under the accelerated cost recovery system, assets are assigned to one of four classes, with standard tax lives of 3, 5, 10, or 15 years. By 1986, assets in the first three classes can be depreciated at a 200 percent declining balance rate. Also, a 25 percent tax credit now is granted for new R&D spending above the annual figure averaged over the past three years.

The U.S. corporate income tax rate on earnings greater than $100,000 became 46 percent, effective in taxable years beginning after December 31, 1978.

Appendix A

TABLE A-2. GRANTS AND CAPITAL SUBSIDIES, 1978

	Regional Focus	Industrial Focus
Canada	Manufacturing and processing industries eligible for cash grants in designated areas, generally limited to $5,000 per direct job created or ¼ capital cost, new plant and equipment.	Industrial adjustment assistance for footwear and tanning.
France	Industrial subsidies up to ¼ capital costs and/or FF 25,000 per job created, dependent on region of country. Additional subsidies and variable rate loans under special Fund for Industrial Adaptation covering investment in very specific areas of high unemployment. Subsidies treated as taxable income spread over life of depreciable assets.	Grants available for engineering or data processing activities regardless of initial investment, up to FF 25,000 per job created in certain areas.
Germany	Investment premium of 7.5% of cost of new depreciable assets used to establish business in new development areas, 10% premium in West Berlin. Additional grants up to 18.5% on eastern border and 30% in West Berlin may be approved.	Investment premium of 7.5% of cost of new depreciable assets used for R&D or production and distribution of energy.
Italy	Grants for capital investment in southern Italy, 40% for investments up to $2.3 million, scaled down to 15% for amounts greater than $17 million. Can be increased further, ⅙ for special sectors or particularly depressed regions. Subsidized interest rates, 30% of reference rate (15.75% in Dec. '77) up to 40% of investments less than $17 million. Less generous provisions for certain small-scale investments in central and northern Italy.	Revolving industrial research fund, 40% to be allocated to south, 20% to small businesses. Subsidized loans, contribution to expenditures, and direct equity participation.
Japan		Employment Stabilization Fund to aid depressed sectors, plus guaranteed loans and capital subsidies.
United Kingdom	Regional development grants 20-22% value of capital expenditure, depending on location, without reducing depreciable value. In Northern Ireland, capital grants of 30-40%, selective employment payment of £2 weekly per full-time worker. Loans at concessionary rates.	National Economic Development Council aid to sectors to promote modernization and new product developments (£350 million to 15 sectors) particularly to expand exports and reduce import dependence. National Enterprise Board equity participation.
United States		Trade adjustment assistance measures for trade impacted workers and firms.

APPENDIX B.
Modeling International Competitive Effects of Tax and Subsidy Policies

To assess the effect of tax and subsidy policies in competitive markets where producers adjust output in response to changes in market prices, a basic starting point is to specify the supply and demand functions in all relevant markets. The resulting model is explained with respect to world steel trade, although it is also applied in analyzing world automotive markets in this study. An approach developed by Armington is applied, which assumes that products from different countries are not perfect substitutes for each other.[1] Rather, differences in quality and reliability of delivery distinguish even standardized products such as steel, where no single world price can be applied to the output of all countries. Therefore, to analyze changing market shares in the steel industry, attention must be paid to production in separate competing national markets. All purchasers of a given national output are assumed to be charged the same price, which rules out possible price discrimination between home customers and export sales. While such discrimination in fact may take place, it reflects other factors that allow producers to segment markets and is not a direct consequence of government output subsidies. Also, attention here is focused on the substitutability between the steel produced by different countries, and consequently the prices of commodities competing with steel, such as tin, are assumed to remain constant.

The major interest in this study is to assess how foreign tax and subsidy practices affect U.S. producers. Consequently, if major subsidy policies were pursued in two countries, X and Y, then it would be necessary to examine supply and demand conditions in the markets for output from the United States, country X and Y and the rest of the world, R. By setting the change in quantity supplied equal to the change in quantity demanded in each of these markets, the change in price that occurs in each separate market in response to the initial subsidy policies of X and Y can be calculated. All four markets must be included to capture how price reductions offered by X and Y producers will reduce sales of producers in the United States and the rest of the world. These producers, in turn, will be able to sell at lower prices as they cut back their use of high-cost peak capacity plants. The extent of those price reductions will determine how much sales by the rest of the world are reduced in countries X and Y and how easily they can recapture those sales by diverting output to the U.S. market.

The arithmetic solution to this set of price changes is as follows:

$$(1)\ E_{US} \cdot \frac{dP_{US}}{P_{US}} = \theta_{US}^{US} \left[N_{US-US}^{US} \cdot \frac{dP_{US}}{P_{US}} + N_{US-X}^{US} \cdot \frac{dP_X}{P_X} + N_{US-Y}^{US} \cdot \frac{dP_Y}{P_Y} + N_{US-R}^{US} \cdot \frac{dP_R}{P_R} \right]$$

$$+ \theta_R^{US} \left[N_{US-US}^{R} \cdot \frac{dP_{US}}{P_{US}} + N_{US-X}^{R} \cdot \frac{dP_X}{P_X} + N_{US-Y}^{R} \cdot \frac{dP_Y}{P_Y} + N_{US-R}^{R} \cdot \frac{dP_R}{P_R} \right]$$

$$(2)\ E_X \left(\frac{dP_X}{P_X} + \phi_X \right) = \theta_{US}^{X} \left[N_{X-US}^{US} \cdot \frac{dP_{US}}{P_{US}} + N_{X-X}^{US} \cdot \frac{dP_X}{P_X} + N_{X-Y}^{US} \cdot \frac{dP_Y}{P_Y} + N_{X-R}^{US} \cdot \frac{dP_R}{P_R} \right]$$

$$+ \theta_X^{X} \left[N_{X-US}^{X} \cdot \frac{dP_{US}}{P_{US}} + N_{X-X}^{X} \cdot \frac{dP_X}{P_X} + N_{X-Y}^{X} \cdot \frac{dP_Y}{P_Y} + N_{X-R}^{X} \cdot \frac{dP_R}{P_R} \right]$$

$$+ \theta_Y^{X} \left[N_{X-US}^{Y} \cdot \frac{dP_{US}}{P_{US}} + N_{X-X}^{Y} \cdot \frac{dP_X}{P_X} + N_{X-Y}^{Y} \cdot \frac{dP_Y}{P_Y} + N_{X-R}^{Y} \cdot \frac{dP_R}{P_R} \right]$$

$$+ \theta_R^{X} \left[N_{X-US}^{R} \cdot \frac{dP_{US}}{P_{US}} + N_{X-X}^{R} \cdot \frac{dP_X}{P_X} + N_{X-Y}^{R} \cdot \frac{dP_Y}{P_Y} + N_{X-R}^{R} \cdot \frac{dP_R}{P_R} \right]$$

$$(3)\ E_Y \left(\frac{dP_Y}{P_Y} + \phi_Y \right) = \theta_{US}^{Y} \left[N_{Y-US}^{US} \cdot \frac{dP_{US}}{P_{US}} + N_{Y-X}^{US} \cdot \frac{dP_X}{P_X} + N_{Y-Y}^{US} \cdot \frac{dP_Y}{P_Y} + N_{Y-R}^{US} \cdot \frac{dP_R}{P_R} \right]$$

$$+ \theta_X^{Y} \left[N_{Y-US}^{X} \cdot \frac{dP_{US}}{P_{US}} + N_{Y-X}^{X} \cdot \frac{dP_X}{P_X} + N_{Y-Y}^{X} \cdot \frac{dP_Y}{P_Y} + N_{Y-R}^{X} \cdot \frac{dP_R}{P_R} \right]$$

$$+ \theta_Y^{Y} \left[N_{Y-US}^{Y} \cdot \frac{dP_{US}}{P_{US}} + N_{Y-X}^{Y} \cdot \frac{dP_X}{P_X} + N_{Y-Y}^{Y} \cdot \frac{dP_Y}{P_Y} + N_{Y-R}^{Y} \cdot \frac{dP_R}{P_R} \right]$$

Appendix B

$$(4) \quad E_R \cdot \frac{dP_R}{P_R} = \theta_{US}^R \left[N_{R-US}^{US} \cdot \frac{dP_{US}}{P_{US}} + N_{R-X}^{US} \cdot \frac{dP_X}{P_X} + N_{R-Y}^{US} \cdot \frac{dP_Y}{P_Y} + N_{R-R}^{US} \cdot \frac{dP_R}{P_R} \right]$$

$$+ \theta_R^Y \left[N_{Y-US}^R \cdot \frac{dP_{US}}{P_{US}} + N_{Y-X}^R \cdot \frac{dP_X}{P_X} + N_{Y-Y}^R \cdot \frac{dP_Y}{P_Y} + N_{Y-R}^R \cdot \frac{dP_R}{P_R} \right]$$

$$+ \theta_X^R \left[N_{R-US}^X \cdot \frac{dP_{US}}{P_{US}} + N_{R-X}^X \cdot \frac{dP_X}{P_X} + N_{R-Y}^X \cdot \frac{dP_Y}{P_Y} + N_{R-R}^X \cdot \frac{dP_R}{P_R} \right]$$

$$+ \theta_Y^R \left[N_{R-US}^Y \cdot \frac{dP_{US}}{P_{US}} + N_{R-X}^Y \cdot \frac{dP_X}{P_X} + N_{R-Y}^Y \cdot \frac{dP_Y}{P_Y} + N_{R-R}^Y \cdot \frac{dP_R}{P_R} \right]$$

$$+ \theta_R^R \left[N_{R-US}^R \cdot \frac{dP_{US}}{P_{US}} + N_{R-X}^R \cdot \frac{dP_X}{P_X} + N_{R-Y}^R \cdot \frac{dP_Y}{P_Y} + N_{R-R}^R \cdot \frac{dP_R}{P_R} \right]$$

where $\frac{dP_i}{P_i}$ is the change in price of country i's output, ϕ_i is the subsidy paid by country i as a percentage of the initial market price, E_i is the elasticity of supply in country i, θ_j^i shows the portion of country i's output sold in market j, and N_{jk}^i indicates the elasticity of demand in country i for output from country j with respect to a change in price by country k.

Values for these various cross-price elasticities of demand can be obtained in Armington's framework as follows:

$$(5) \quad N_{jk}^i = s_k^i (\sigma_i - N_i)$$

$$(6) \quad N_{jj}^i = (1 - s_j^i) \sigma_i - s_j^i N_i$$

where s_j^i reflects the share of country i's market accounted for by country j, σ_i is the common elasticity of substitution between the various national products traded, and N_i is the price elasticity of demand for an aggregate measure of all steel.

These expressions demonstrate one of the key points mentioned in the text, that a subsidy in a country that has a small market share will not greatly affect world trade and output, even though that country's price and output can change substantially from its small initial base. In other words, the elasticity of demand for output from the subsidized country may be fairly large, but the cross-price elasticity of demand for other goods with respect to a change in the subsidized price will be small.

Because the majority of the elasticity values shown in equations (1) to (4) are not commonly estimated in empirical studies, equations (5) and (6) must be used to calculate them. Market share data are commonly available, and therefore knowing the proper values for the elasticities of substitution, σ_i, and the elasticity of demand for the entire commodity branch, N_i, provides a sufficient base of information. For the application of the model to the steel industry, all countries are assumed to have the same elasticity of demand for steel, equal to -0.25, as reported by the FTC. With respect to the elasticity of substitution, σ_i, Jondrow reports a short-run estimate of 1.0 and a long-run estimate of 6.0 for the United States.[2] Corresponding figures for the European countries are derived from estimated values for import elasticities of demand reported by Humphrey.[3] With respect to supply elasticities, the value of 0.6 used in the FTC study is adopted. Alternative values of both these supply and demand parameters were utilized, but in none of the cases simulated did the projected impact on U.S. labor become large.

Notes

1   Paul Armington, "A theory of demand for products distinguished by place of origin," *International Monetary Fund Staff Papers*, Vol. 16 (1969), pp. 159–177.

2   James Jondrow, "Effects of trade restrictions on imports of steel," in *The Impact of International Trade and Investment on Employment*, ed. W. Dewald (Washington, D.C., 1978), pp. 11–25.

3   D.H. Humphrey, "Disaggregated Import Functions for the U.K., West Germany and France," *Oxford Bulletin of Economics and Statistics*, Vol. 38 (November 1976), pp. 281–298.

APPENDIX C.
Assessing a Proposed Value-Added Tax

Another key issue with respect to general tax policy in the United States has been resurgent interest in the adoption of a general value-added tax. Many proponents tout its more neutral effects compared to the current tax structure of the United States. Other allegations have centered on the possible international competitive effects of such a change in U.S. tax structure. While many other aspects of a VAT are relevant as well, the major assumptions of these two arguments are evaluated here.

THE IMPACT ON TRADE PATTERNS

The balance of trade argument has received considerable attention, but considerable confusion still remains. An important starting point in addressing the issue of trade effects of tax policy and border-tax adjustments is the Tinbergen Report of 1953.[1] Border-tax adjustments refer to the way taxes are imposed or rebated when goods flow into or out of a country. Under the origin principle, no adjustments are made at the border, and the relevant tax burden is that imposed in the country where the good originates. Under the destination principle, the tax is rebated on exports and imposed on imports; taxes are paid on goods in the country where they are consumed regardless of whether they are produced there or imported. The Tinbergen Report dealt with European tax harmonization and the possible bias from applying the destination principle or the origin principle to indirect taxes. The report concluded that the choice of BTA did not matter where a general tax was concerned. For instance, if an indirect tax were levied under the destination principle, relative prices internationally would not be altered because the tax would be rebated on exports and imposed on imports. If the origin principle were applied, then relative prices internationally would be affected because the taxing country would not rebate the tax on exports or apply the tax to imports. Exports would be less competitive and imports would become more attractive than domestic goods. To eliminate this trade deficit, a depreciation of the taxing country's currency would occur, which would exactly offset the general price distortion created initially. The same world trade patterns would exist in either situation, and therefore the choice of BTA is not important. This position has been restated more recently by Whalley: "In long-run equilibrium a movement from a destination to an origin principle will affect only the exchange rate. No effect on real trade flows will result, and no trade advantage is involved."[2]

The Tinbergen conclusion has been challenged on various grounds, though. For instance, when unbalanced trade and international financial flows are added to the analysis, then any exchange-rate change affects not just trade flows but also capital transactions. If Germany had shifted from the origin principle to the destination principle of BTA, the resulting trade surplus would require an appreciation of the German mark. This appreciation would mean that earnings from foreign currency bond holdings, for example, would translate into fewer marks. Thus, part of the reduction in the balance-of-payments surplus would have occurred on the capital account and not entirely on the trade account.

Alternatively, consider capital equipment instead of financial claims. When capital can move internationally and the location of production can be altered, the simple neutrality proposition also breaks down. Increasing an indirect tax levied according to the origin principle results in a trade deficit for the taxing region, which is offset by the earnings of capital that leaves the country.[3] The situation differs from the Tinbergen analysis because all adjustment is not assumed to occur through changes in the prices of goods internationally, since capital services can be traded as well as goods. In terms of recent proposals to cut the U.S. corporate income tax and instead to impose a VAT to yield the same revenue, the incentive to produce outside the United States would be reduced, total earnings from foreign investments would decline, and the U.S. trade balance would improve. In other words, the improvement in the trade balance mirrors the reduction in foreign investment earnings, which results because new investments are directed toward the United States to a greater extent.

Finally, another objection to the Tinbergen type conclusion regarding the neutrality of alternative BTAs has been raised by Grossman with respect to current European VATs.[4] He points out that most imported goods are not sold to final consumers but rather as intermediate goods. If the GATT were to apply the origin principle instead of the destination principle on indirect taxes, the price of exports would increase, but the trade-off between imports and domestic goods made by home producers and retailers would not be affected. Imported intermediate goods do not become more attractive even though the tax levied on domestic intermediate goods is not levied on them. The reason is that the purchaser can claim a credit for the indirect tax already paid by the domestic producer. Because exports do become relatively less attractive under the origin principle, an exchange depreciation must occur. But this depreciation would be smaller than the proportional VAT, resulting in a reduction in the total volume of trade. Grossman's estimates of the quantitative impact of switching to the origin principle are that French exports to the United States would fall by 14 to 21 percent, German exports to the United States by 9 to 13 percent, and U.K. exports to the United States by 5 to 8 percent.

These various qualifications to the Tinbergen Report suggest that the choice of BTA principle *does* make a difference to the pattern of world production and trade.

SECTORAL NEUTRALITY OF A VAT

The second issue to be considered here is that a switch from current direct taxes to a general VAT would be desirable, aside from any balance of trade claims. For instance, the corporate income tax leads to an increase in the relative price of goods produced by the corporate sector, and the higher the tax rate, the greater the relative disadvantage. A reduction in the corporate income tax rate, or a liberalization of depreciation allowances, or an increase in the investment tax credit that can be claimed all reduce the effective corporate tax rate and reduce this distortion. Of course, choices among these alternative tax reduction measures do have different effects across industries as some sectors require more long-lived capital, others are more risky and require greater equity financing, and others are more labor intensive.

Alternatively, a reduction in the social security tax that does not merely result in higher real wages probably offers the greatest benefit to labor-intensive goods. To predict the precise effect of any tax cutback would require more attention to what changes in the social security tax were contemplated: a decrease in the basic rate or a reduction in the ceiling level of income to be taxed. The latter change might have even more effect on capital-intensive industries that hire more highly paid laborers.

Reducing either the corporate income tax or the social security tax would eliminate a current source of inefficiency in the U.S. economy. Would imposing a VAT to collect a comparable amount of revenue create any other distortions or favor any particular sectors of the economy? The impact of a VAT would depend on the choice of tax base and the uniformity of the tax rate applied. Most proponents of a VAT in the United States favor a consumption-based tax as a way of encouraging investment.[5] If the imposition of a VAT were coupled with a reduction in the corporate income tax, demand likely would shift in favor of capital goods production and away from consumer goods. While the goal of increased investment might be achieved, labor-force participation might fall in reaction to the fall in real value of wages caused by the increased VAT. Thus, the consumption-based VAT should not be regarded as a perfectly distortion-free alternative to the present tax structure. Rather, the more appropriate argument is that these new distortions are likely to be smaller than the capital inefficiencies being removed.

Aside from these issues with respect to the proper tax base, European experience with the VAT suggests that differential impacts across consumer goods will be felt. For instance, using figures from 1975, the French basic rate of 20 percent was raised to 33 percent on luxury products and reduced to 17.6 percent on energy sources and forest products and 7 percent on most foodstuffs and agricultural products. The German rate of 11 percent was reduced to 5.5 percent for food supplies and professional services. In the Italian case, the basic rate of 12 percent was reduced to 6 percent on agricultural products, foods, pharmaceuticals, books, and textile products, and raised up to 30 percent for luxury products such as cars with engines greater than 2000 cc. The British standard rate of 8 percent was reduced to zero for food, books, construction, and transport. Therefore, past experience with the VAT abroad, as well as coverage of state sales taxes in the United States, suggests that a general VAT, even with respect to consumer goods, is unlikely to be imposed. Largely for equity reasons, some goods will be favored more than others. Perhaps the way these different rates must be established legislatively makes lawmakers more aware of the differential impact in these cases than when corporate tax changes are debated.

A final aspect of this discussion that warrants further underscoring is that simply adopting a VAT in the United States results in no relative trade advantage, unless private citizens value the additional government expenditure more than their own private purchases, or if other taxes are reduced, thereby avoiding an overall increase in government spending. Otherwise, the lower real income of Americans again is likely to have adverse effects on labor-force participation, real saving and economic growth.

Notes

1   More formally, see European Coal and Steel Community, High Authority, *Report on the Problems Raised by the Different Turnover Tax Systems Applied Within the Common Market* (1953).

2   John Whalley, "Tax Developments Outside the United States and Their Implications for Current U.S. Reform Proposals," in *Federal Tax Reform: Myths and Realities* (San Francisco: Institute for Contemporary Studies, 1978), p. 228.

3   For a review of these recent developments, see Carlos Longo, "Tax Coordination under Benefit Taxation," *National Tax Journal,* Vol. 31, No. 4 (December 1978), pp. 385–389.

4   Gene Grossman, "Border Tax Adjustments, Do They Distort Trade?" *Journal of International Economics,* Vol. 10, No. 1 (1980), pp. 117–128.

5   European countries impose consumption-type VATs, which mean that the VAT paid on all input purchases in a period, including capital goods, is deducted from the VAT due on a firm's sales of output during the period. Alternatively, an income-type VAT would require that the VAT paid on purchases of capital goods be amortized over the life of the asset and credited against the VAT due on sales for successive periods (D. Smith, J. Webber and C. Cerf, *What You Should Know about the Value Added Tax* (Homewood, Ill.: Dow Jones–Irwin, 1973). Compared to the consumption-type VAT, the income-type VAT acts as a deterrent to investment. Another way of avoiding that deterrent would be through the adoption of an expenditure tax instead of an income tax. Thus, a proponent of greater investment incentives still might not favor a VAT as the best means of making up any revenue shortfall from reducing taxes on capital income.

Selected Bibliography

Armington, Paul. "A theory of demand for products distinguished by place of origin." *International Monetary Fund Staff Papers*. 1969, pp. 159-177.
British Steel Corporation. *Annual Report and Accounts 1978-1979*. London. 1979.
Commission of the European Communities. *Grants and Loans from the European Community*. Brussels. 1979.
———. *Second Report on Competition Policy*. Brussels. 1973.
———. *Fourth Report on Competition Policy*. Brussels. 1975.
———. *Fifth Report on Competition Policy*. Brussels. 1976.
———. *Sixth Report on Competition Policy*. Brussels. 1977.
———. *Eighth Report on Competition Policy*. Brussels. 1979.
———. *Twelfth Report on the Activities of the European Community*. Brussels. 1979.
Cooper, R.N. "U.S. Policies and Practices on Subsidies in International Trade." In *International Trade and Industrial Policies*. Ed. Steven Warnecke. New York: Holmes and Meier. 1978, pp. 107-122.
Economic Planning Agency. *New Economic and Social Seven-Year Plan*. Tokyo: Foreign Press Center, 1979.
Electronic Data Processing Japan Reports. Tokyo. 1978.
European Coal and Steel Community, High Authority. *Report on the Problems Raised by the Different Turnover Tax Systems Applied Within the Common Market*. Brussels. 1953.
"European Strategies to Fight IBM." *Business Week*, December 17, 1979, pp. 73-76.
"The 500 Largest Industrial Corporations Outside of the U.S." *Fortune*, August 13, 1979, pp. 194-203.
"Giscard steels himself for nationalization." *The Economist*, September 23, 1978, p. 95.
Grossman, Gene. "Border Tax Adjustments, Do They Distort Trade?" *Journal of International Economics*, 10 (February 1980). pp. 117-128.
Harman, Alvin. *The International Computer Industry*. Cambridge, Mass.: Harvard University Press. 1971.
Horst, Thomas. *Income Taxation and Competitiveness*. Washington, D.C.: National Planning Association. 1977.
Hufbauer, Gary. "The Taxation of Export Profits." *National Tax Journal*, 28 (March 1975). pp. 43-60.
James, Barrie G. *The Future of the Multinational Pharmaceutical Industry to 1990*. New York: John Wiley. 1977.
Johnson, Chalmers. *Japan's Public Policy Companies*. Washington, D.C.: American Enterprise Institute. 1978.
Jondrow, James. "Effects of trade restrictions on imports of steel." In *The Impact of International Trade and Investment on Employment*. Ed. W. Dewald. Washington, D.C.: GPO. 1978, pp. 11-25.
Kamiya, Shotaro. *My Life with Toyota*. Japan: Toyota Motor Sales Company, Ltd. 1976.
Kaplan, Eugene. *Japan, the Government-Business Relationship*. Washington, D.C.: U.S. Department of Commerce. 1972.
Keesing, Donald and Martin Wolf. *Textile Quotas Against Developing Countries*. London: Trade Policy Research Center. 1980.
Kopits, George. *International Comparison of Tax Depreciation Practices*. Paris: Organization for Economic Cooperation and Development. 1975.

Krauss, M.B. "Quantification of the Effects of Non-tariff Barriers in the Major Trading Countries." Report J9K60025 submitted to U.S. Department of Labor. 1978.

Lecht, Charles. *The Waves of Change.* New York: McGraw-Hill. 1977.

Longo, Carlos. "Tax Coordination under Benefit Taxation." *National Tax Journal,* 31 (December 1978). pp. 385–389.

Marketing Guide to the Pharmaceutical Industry. Westport, Conn.: Technomic Publishing. 1970.

McCulloch, Rachel. *Research and Development as a Determinant of U.S. International Competitiveness.* Washington, D.C.: National Planning Association. 1978.

Miles, Caroline. "Protection of the British Textile Industry." In *Public Assistance to Industry, Protection and Subsidies in Britain and Germany.* Eds. W.M. Corden and G. Fels. Boulder: Westview Press. 1976, pp. 184–213.

Ministry of International Trade and Industry. *Japan's Industrial Structure—A Long Range Vision,* 1978 Edition. Tokyo. 1978.

Neihaus, Robert. *The Canada-Ford Deal.* Washington, D.C.: Northeast-Midwest Institute. 1978.

Neu, Axel. "Protection of the German Textile Industry." In *Public Assistance to Industry.* Eds. W.M. Corden and G. Fels. Boulder: Westview Press. 1976, pp. 165–183.

Organization for Economic Cooperation and Development. *Policies for the Stimulation of Industrial Innovation.* Volume II. Paris. 1978.

———. *Selected Industrial Policy Instrument, Objectives and Scope.* Paris. 1978.

———. *The 1978 Tax/Benefit Position of a Typical Worker in OECD Member Countries.* Paris. 1979.

Pechman, Joseph and Keimei Kaizuka. "Taxation." In *Asia's New Giant.* Eds. Hugh Patrick and Henry Rosovsky. Washington, D.C.: Brookings Institution. 1976, pp. 317–382.

Pestieau, Caroline. *The Canadian Textile Policy: A Sectoral Trade Adjustment Strategy?* Quebec: C.D. Howe Research Institute. 1976.

Pharmaceutical Manufacturers' Association. *Annual Survey Report 1978-1979.* Washington, D.C. 1980.

"Public Sector Enterprise." *The Economist,* December 30, 1978, pp. 38–61.

Putnam, Hayes and Bartlett, Inc. *Economics of International Steel Trade.* Newton, Massachusetts. 1977.

Schwarzman, David. *Innovation in the Pharmaceutical Industry.* Baltimore: Johns Hopkins University Press. 1976.

Smith, D., J. Webber and C. Cerf. *What You Should Know About the Value Added Tax.* Homewood, Ill.: Dow Jones-Irwin. 1973.

Soma, John. *The Computer Industry, An Economic-Legal Analysis of its Technology and Growth.* Lexington, Mass.: D.C. Heath. 1976.

U.S. Congress. House Committee on Ways and Means. Subcommittee on Trade. *Background Materials on the Trade Adjustment Assistance Programs under Title II of the Trade Act of 1974.* 95th Cong., 1st sess. WMCP: 95-17. Washington, D.C.: GPO. 1977.

———. *Background Materials on the Multifiber Agreement.* 95th Cong., 2nd sess. WMCP: 95-62. Washington, D.C.: GPO. 1978.

U.S. Congress. Office of Technology Assessment. *Technology and Steel Industry Competitiveness.* Washington, D.C.: GPO. 1980.

U.S. Department of Commerce. *Sharpening Government Response to Plant Closings.* Washington, D.C. 1979.

U.S. Department of the Treasury. *The Operation and Effect of the Domestic International Sales Corporation Legislation,* 1977 Annual Report. Washington, D.C. 1978.

———. *The Operation and Effect of the Possessions' Corporation System of Taxation.* Washington, D.C.: GPO. 1978.

U.S. Federal Trade Commission. *Staff Report on the United States Steel Industry and Its International Rivals.* Washington, D.C. 1977.

Walters, Kenneth and Joseph Monsen. "State-owned business abroad: new competitive threat." *Harvard Business Review,* 57 (March–April 1979). pp. 160–170.

Wardell, W. and L. Lasagna. *Regulation and Drug Development.* Washington, D.C.: American Enterprise Institute. 1975.

Warnecke, Steven. "The European Community and National Subsidy Policies." In *International Trade and Industrial Policies*. Ed. Steven Warnecke. New York: Holmes and Meier. 1978, pp. 143–174.

Whalley, John. "Tax Developments Outside the United States and Their Implications for Current U.S. Reform Proposals." In *Federal Tax Reform: Myths and Realities*. San Francisco: Institute for Contemporary Studies. 1978, pp. 211–232.

Whiting, A. "Overseas Experience in the Use of Industrial Subsidies." In *The Economics of Industrial Subsidies*. Ed. Alan Whiting. Department of Industry, London: HMSO. 1976, pp. 45–63.

NPA

NPA is an independent, private, nonprofit, nonpolitical organization that carries on research and policy formulation in the public interest. NPA was founded during the Great Depression of the 1930s when conflicts among the major economic groups—business, labor, agriculture—threatened to paralyze national decisionmaking on the critical issues confronting American society. It was dedicated to the task of getting these diverse groups to work together to narrow areas of controversy and broaden areas of agreement and to provide on specific problems concrete programs for action planned in the best traditions of a functioning democracy. Such democratic planning, NPA believes, involves the development of effective governmental and private policies and programs not only by official agencies but also through the independent initiative and cooperation of the main private-sector groups concerned. And, to preserve and strengthen American political and economic democracy, the necessary government actions have to be consistent with, and stimulate the support of, a dynamic private sector.

NPA brings together influential and knowledgeable leaders from business, labor, agriculture, and the applied and academic professions to serve on policy committees. These committees identify emerging problems confronting the nation at home and abroad and seek to develop and agree upon policies and programs for coping with them. The research and writing for these committees are provided by NPA's professional staff and, as required, by outside experts.

In addition, NPA's professional staff undertakes research designed to provide data and ideas for policymakers and planners in government and the private sector. These activities include the preparation on a regular basis of economic and demographic projections for the national economy, regions, states, metropolitan areas, and counties; research on national goals and priorities, productivity and economic growth, welfare and dependency problems, employment and manpower needs, energy and environmental questions, and other economic and social problems confronting American society; and analyses and forecasts of changing international realities and their implications for U.S. policies. In developing its staff capabilities, NPA has increasingly emphasized two related qualifications. First is the development of the interdisciplinary knowledge required to understand the complex nature of many real-life problems. Second is the ability to bridge the gap between theoretical or highly technical research and the practical needs of policymakers and planners in government and the private sector.

All NPA reports have been authorized for publication in accordance with procedures laid down by the Board of Trustees. Such action does not imply agreement by NPA board or committee members with all that is contained therein unless such endorsement is specifically stated.

NPA Officers and Board of Trustees

WALTER STERLING SURREY
Chairman; Senior Partner, Surrey and Morse

MURRAY H. FINLEY
Chairman of the Executive Committee; President, Amalgamated Clothing & Textile Workers' Union

DALE HOOVER
Vice Chairman-Agriculture; Professor of Economics, Department of Economics, North Carolina State University

JOSEPH D. KEENAN
Vice Chairman-Labor; Washington, D.C.

JOHN MILLER
Vice Chairman and Acting President; NPA

RICHARD WARREN WHEELER
Treasurer; Senior Vice President, Citibank, N.A.

WILLIAM W. WINPISINGER
Secretary; President, International Association of Machinists & Aerospace Workers

NEIL J. McMULLEN
Executive Vice President-International; NPA

SPERRY LEA
Vice President; NPA

NESTOR TERLECKYJ
Vice President; NPA

CLARK C. ABT
President, Abt Associates Inc.

W.B. BEHNKE
Vice Chairman, Commonwealth Edison

PHILIP BRIGGS
Executive Vice President, Metropolitan Life Insurance Company

ROBERT K. BUCK
Waukee, Iowa

EDWARD J. CARLOUGH
General President, Sheet Metal Workers' International Association

SOL C. CHAIKIN
President, International Ladies' Garment Workers' Union

J.G. CLARKE
Director and Senior Vice President, Exxon Corporation

JACOB CLAYMAN
President, National Council of Senior Citizens, Inc.

G.A. COSTANZO
New York, New York

EDWARD L. CUSHMAN
Clarence Hilberry University Professor, Wayne State University

JOHN DIEBOLD
Chairman, The Diebold Group, Inc.

THOMAS W. diZEREGA
President, Northwest Energy Company

STEPHEN C. EYRE
Senior Vice President-Secretary, Citibank, N.A.

DOUGLAS A. FRASER
President, International Union, United Automobile, Aerospace & Agricultural Implement Workers of America-UAW

ROBERT M. FREDERICK
Legislative Director, National Grange

ROBERT R. FREDERICK
Executive Vice President & Sector Executive of International Sector, General Electric Company

THEODORE GEIGER
Distinguished Research Professor of Intersocietal Relations, School of Foreign Service, Georgetown University

RALPH W. GOLBY
Vice President-Investor Relations, Schering-Plough Corporation

PHILIP HAMMER
Palm Harbor, Florida

TERRY HERNDON
Executive Director, National Education Association

G. GRIFFITH JOHNSON, JR.
Executive Vice President, Motion Picture Association of America, Inc.

PETER T. JONES
Senior Vice President and General Counsel, Levi Strauss & Company

LANE KIRKLAND
President, AFL-CIO

JUANITA KREPS
Durham, North Carolina

PETER KROGH
Dean, School of Foreign Service, Georgetown University

JOHN H. LYONS
General President, International Association of Bridge, Structural and Ornamental Iron Workers

LLOYD McBRIDE
International President, United Steelworkers of America, AFL-CIO, CLC

WILLIAM J. McDONOUGH
Chairman, Asset and Liability Management Committee,
The First National Bank of Chicago

JOHN W. MACY, JR.
McLean, Virginia

FRANK D. MARTINO
President, Chemical Workers Union International

WILLIAM R. MILLER
Executive Vice President, Bristol-Myers Company

WILLIAM G. MITCHELL
President, Central Telephone & Utilities Corporation

HARRY E. MORGAN, JR.
Senior Vice President, Weyerhaeuser Company

RODNEY W. NICHOLS
Executive Vice President, The Rockefeller University

WILLIAM S. OGDEN
Vice Chairman and Chief Financial Officer, The Chase Manhattan Bank, N.A.

WILLIAM R. PEARCE
Corporate Vice President, Cargill Incorporated

GEORGE POULIN
Corporate Vice President, International Association of Machinists & Aerospace Workers

S. FRANK RAFTERY
General President, International Brotherhood of Painters & Allied Trades

RALPH RAIKES
Ashland, Nebraska

JOHN S. REED
Senior Executive Vice President, Citibank, N.A.

CARL E. REICHARDT
President, Wells Fargo Bank

WILLIAM D. ROGERS
Partner, Arnold and Porter

STANLEY H. RUTTENBERG
President, Ruttenberg, Friedman, Kilgallon, Gutchess & Associates, Inc.

HOWARD D. SAMUEL
President, Industrial Union Department, AFL-CIO

REX A. SEBASTIAN
Senior Vice President-Operations, Dresser Industries, Inc.

RICHARD J. SCHMEELK
Partner, Salomon Brothers

LAUREN K. SOTH
Journalist, West Des Moines, Iowa

MILAN STONE
URW International President, United Rubber, Cork, Linoleum and Plastic Workers of America, AFL-CIO, CLC

J.C. TURNER
General President, International Union of Operating Engineers, AFL-CIO

THOMAS N. URBAN
President, Pioneer Hi-Bred International

MARTIN J. WARD
General President, United Association of Journeymen and Apprentices of the Plumbing and Pipe Fitting Industry of the United States and Canada

GLENN E. WATTS
President, Communications Workers of America, AFL-CIO

WILLIAM L. WEARLY
Chairman, Executive Committee, Ingersoll-Rand Company

GEORGE L-P WEAVER
Consultant, ORT Technical Assistance

LLOYD B. WESCOTT
Hunterdon Hills Holsteins, inc.

CHARLES G. WOOTTON
Senior Director, Foreign and Domestic Analysis and Planning, Gulf Oil Corporation

WILLIAM H. WYNN
International President, United Food & Commercial Workers International Union, AFL-CIO, CLC

RALPH S. YOHE
Editor, *Wisconsin Agriculturist*

HONORARY TRUSTEES

SOLOMON BARKIN
Department of Economics, University of Massachusetts

LUTHER H. GULICK
Chairman of the Board, Institute of Public Administration

KENNETT W. HINKS
Cockeysville, Maryland

JAMES G. PATTON
Menlo Park, California

LIBRARY OF DAVIDSON COLLEGE

on regular loan may be checked out for **two weeks.** Books
sented at the Circulation Desk in order to be renewed.